Let It Go!

How to Gain Freedom from Your Past and Power for Your Future

Let It Go!

How to Gain Freedom from Your Past and Power for Your Future

Orrin Rudolph

The Gap Closer™

A Gap Closer™ Publication
Life On Purpose Publishing
An Angela Massey Imprint
SAN ANTONIO, TEXAS

Orrin Rudolph
coach@orrinrudolph.com
orrinrudolph.com

Ordering Information:
Quantity sales. Special discounts are available on quantity purchases by corporations, associations, and others. For details, contact the author at the website address above.

Let It Go/Orrin Rudolph. -- 1st ed.
ISBN 978-0-692-13677-5
LCN: 2018947237

Dedication

I dedicate this book first, to the woman I promised my heart and life to, my wonderful wife, Sarah. Without your encouragement, persistence and the occasional loving kick in the pants, this book would not have seen the light of day!

To my beautiful, precious daughters, Salaidh and Siann. There are no words to adequately describe how much love I have for you. You fill my heart and life with indescribable joy.

You are all amazing gifts from my Father which only He could provide so perfectly!

Acknowledgements

As Proverbs 27: 17 says, "As iron sharpens iron, so one person sharpens another." I have found that without many others in my life who have supported me, encouraged me and sharpened me, this vision would never have come to fruition. Some have played an active, conscious part, others were observed from afar and still others were unaware participants on this journey.

I am thrilled to be working with Dr. Angela Massey and Life On Purpose Publishing, and so grateful for your tireless efforts to make this project a success. I have learned so much from you during this process which I know will be an invaluable resource for all the books yet to be birthed.

My deep and abiding gratitude goes out to John Sheasby. Without your incredible teachings on the New Covenant, Grace and the Father's love and your powerful teaching series on forgiveness, this book would not be complete. Your deep insights helped me tremendously and gave me the tools to knit together the "For Christian Eyes Only' section. Thank you for graciously allowing me to use your stories and spiritual insights. They fitted so seamlessly and beautifully into the framework of this book and expounded on the beauty of the Father's forgiveness and our response to it. Without your teaching I would still be wearing 'Grave Clothes."

A special thank you to Dr. Leslie Pollock. Your professional opinions, insights and objective advice has been invaluable. Our discussions at the beach house and on the farm in sunny Australia were a highlight to me and helped me mold some important ideas for this project.

To the many spiritual fathers and mothers over the course of my life who have taught me so much when it comes to life, God and family: Pastor Marius Gradwell, Pastor Errol Peterson and Pastor Rob Dutton, thank you! There are two couples in particular I would like to thank.

First, Pastors Roy and Elize Buck: Thank you for all the love and care you showed me and my family over the years. I see you and your ministry in my life during my formative years as instrumental in helping me become the man I am today. This book has within its pages many life lessons I gleaned from your marriage, ministry and the way you dealt with others. Second, Pastors Gary and Linda Marrone: You became the family we so desperately needed when so far away from our family back in South Africa and Australia. Our long fireside chats and spiritual insights helped unlock revelation upon revelation.

Thank you to Handre deJongh, we met at college and became friends for life. Your wisdom, friendship and encouragement has played a huge part in the realization of this project.

To my parents, Eldin and Lyn Rudolph who have sacrificed, loved, and cared for me without expecting anything in return. Your sacrifices and love are built into the fabric of the pages of this book. I never viewed you as perfect but after becoming a parent I now know that kids don't need perfect, they need love. And you gave that to me in bucket loads.

My deepest love and gratitude to my sister, Candice Rudolph, for loving me even when our relationship was strained. You will always be loved by me.

Finally, my love and gratitude to my beautiful wife Sarah, who without your encouragement, tenacity and support this book would not have seen the light of day.

And all my love to my incredible daughters, Salaidh and Siann. Being your daddy has taught me like nothing else has, the heart of our heavenly Father. It has shown me how to love unconditionally and to forgive without thought of recompense. Your love for me has revealed how love can overcome mistakes and blunders and unlock the heart of a father.

And to my Daddy God. All I have and all I am is because of you. Your love is hidden in these pages like diamonds. There is no forgiveness, no life and no joy without You. And as we are taught by You to *let it go!* we will experience the fullness of Your love more each day.

Praise for *Let It Go!*

"People are always looking for ways to be successful, financially, relationally and health wise. Good work ethics, removing debt, sound business principles, exercise, building a wealth portfolio and saving for the future are all important parts of the success principle. But what many forget is that as long as they are carrying baggage from past hurt and disappointment they are handicapping not only their present but future as well. In *Let it Go!* Orrin Rudolph gives us sound principles and practical advice on how to release the past weight that we tend to carry around with us.

We all need to embrace success without the hindrances and pitfalls from past disappointments and wounds that slow us down. 'Let it Go!' might sound like a catch phrase, but within those simple three words lies the truth and power of freedom. Orrin Rudolph has captured a truth that has been around for eons, but so infrequently used. In order for you to grab hold of a future of joy and success you must first learn to release the chains of the past. In Orrin's words, "don't be afraid to *Let it Go!*"

I have known Orrin for over 26 years since we met our first day in college. I can testify that Orrin is not only writing about the power of forgiveness but has lived through the pain and joy of walking through this process. Applying these principles in your life will lead you to also experience the joy of true freedom and the ability to prosper in all areas of life."

Handre deJongh
Vice President, Global Outreach
Crown Financial Ministries
B.A. Hons Psychology, Harvard Alumni

"In a world scarred by division and rancor, in a society caught in a maelstrom of negativity, with the mainstream media peddling a constant diet of fear, suspicion, and outright character-assassination, where even our comedy has deteriorated into belittling and demeaning ugliness, we need the message of this book to turn the conversation toward healing in our broken society.

The subject of this book, forgiveness and letting go of the baggage of past wounds, has never been more relevant. I am grateful to Orrin for masterfully crafting this important contribution to the restoration of our world to a kinder, gentler place. This message will challenge you and change you as you follow the path that Orrin has laid out toward freedom and wholeness."

John Sheasby
Liberated Living Ministries Inc.
P.O. Box 1350
Glenpool, OK 74033
918-209-5699

"Let it Go! is a powerful reminder of the complications that can control our heart and lives in dealing with unforgiveness. Orrin does an amazing job of being so transparent with sharing his own personal struggles and testimonies of God's true redeeming work of his own Heart and life.

I recommend *Let it Go!* to anyone who has been trying to carry burdens in their own way, the book really takes off when Orrin equips us with God's instructions in how to release us from the weight and burden of unforgiveness forever."

Mike Constantine
CRU Missionary

"Orrin Rudolph is a gifted speaker and presenter and in *Let It Go!* he brings his substantial experience and knowledge of human behaviour to address an issue that is highly relevant in these times, that of forgiveness. Many psychological problems faced by mental health patients are rooted in a lack of skills in dealing with regulating emotions which can lead to poor relationships, anxiety, depression, suicidal thoughts and acts of self-harm.

Forgiveness is one of the skills that is essential to effective relationships and good mental health. In this important book Orrin Rudolph shows how readers can develop an attitude of forgiveness and how this will enhance their everyday lives. This is relevant and essential reading that I recommend."

Dr. Leslie Pollock, Ph.D.
Clinical Psychologist and Service Director
Centre for Psychotherapy
Hunter New England Local Health District, NSW
Australia

Contents

Part Three: The Road to Healing

Part Four: A Road Less Traveled - For Christian Eyes Only!

Part Five: The End of the Road - A Place to Rest

Preface

"Once you let go, you can revel in the euphoria and the weightlessness and freedom that comes with letting go!"
Orrin Rudolph

I read a story once about two monks who were on a pilgrimage. After a long day of travel, they came to a flooded river. At the edge of this river, a young woman sat weeping. The older monk asked the woman what was troubling her. "I'm afraid to cross the river!" she replied. "It is wide, and it is deep and I am afraid I will not make it across without any help." Looking pleadingly at the two monks she begged them to help her. The younger monk turned his back. Their order forbade any of its members to touch a woman. But the older monk, seeing the woman's plight picked her up and without a word, carried her across the swollen river. When reaching the other side, he put her down and continued on his journey. The younger monk was incensed, he began scolding and berating his elder for breaking his vows. This went on for much of the remaining journey.

Finally, a day before reaching their destination the older monk turned to the younger one and quietly said, "I only carried the woman across the river. You have been carrying her this whole journey."

Letting go can be difficult. Letting go of hurt, unmet expectations, disappointments and betrayals are painful, but not as painful as hanging on to them. Every day, every moment presents an opportunity to create ourselves and our futures anew, to shrug off the baggage of the past, open ourselves up to the possibility of the moment and take action to create an incredible future.

It's All About Freedom

I have written this book for two reason.

First, as I have traveled and spoken across the United States and in other countries, I have come across many people and organizations who have asked me to put my seminars into book form so that they would have tools to use. They want tools to get free and remain free of the burdens that they carry.

Second, through utilizing these principles in my counseling sessions, I have seen dramatic results. Many people have come up to me after the seminars to share their stories of emotional weight and how following the principles that I am about to lay out in this book have set them free from these weights that bogged them down for years.

My desire through this is to give you, my reader, the same opportunities these men and woman have had to unbuckle the straps of that burden-filled pack and let it fall to the ground.

Once this happens, you can revel in the euphoria of the weight-lessness and freedom that comes with letting go!

Orrin Rudolph
Longview, Texas
orrinrudolph.com

Part One:

Beginning of the Road –
A Journey of Choice

CHAPTER ONE

The Pack on the Back

"It is truly freedom when we become aware that we have the power and ability to learn new techniques and methods in our responses and not allow ourselves to become victims of our past." Orrin Rudolph

The Amatola Mountain Range in the Eastern Cape Province of South Africa is a remarkable sight. Lush forests, thundering waterfalls, and towering cliffs span its entire length. There is an aspiring Garden of Eden hidden within its depths where small antelope, monkeys, and other varied wildlife enjoy its protective habitat. I became even more aware of its beauty when three of my best friends and I headed out on a Saturday morning in the summer of 1990. We had planned this six-day five-night hiking trip for an entire year and finally, the day had arrived. Six days of nature, six days of nothing but mountains, wildlife, and panoramic views. A time to get away, enjoy nature and each other's company without the daily interruptions of modern life. Each of us measured our packs to perfection, nothing more and nothing less. We packed sleeping bags, food, cooking utensils and everything else we deemed essential to survive on this challenging 65-mile hike, one of the toughest in South Africa.

At 6 a.m., we were dropped off at the starting point of the trail. We slung our packs onto our backs and headed off into the unknown. We were not disappointed, the sights were truly breathtaking from the very beginning, so much so that we almost, and I repeat almost forgot about the weight of the eighty-pound packs on our backs. As the sun began to crest over the horizon, the day became warmer, and our shoulders started to sag under the weight. After about an hour of walking, we decided to take a break and found a grove of large yellowwood trees that created enough shade from the morning sun. We removed the packs and were struck immediately by the feeling of weightless-ness and relief from our heavy burdens. It felt as though we could float away if we were not careful. This feeling created an experi-ence of euphoria and relief that pointed out to us just how burdensome carrying those packs had become. After our short reprieve, we again with reluctance shouldered those cumbersome packs and continued with the day's hike.

I have never forgotten that feeling of that first day's rest stop or the feeling of slowly becoming used to those heavy packs through the next six days of hiking. What amazed me, however, was no matter how accustomed we became to those packs—even to the point where we would not even remove them during our short rest stops—that same euphoria and weightlessness would always accompany their removal. I will never forget something else that stood out to me was the more we got used to those packs on our backs how our desire to remove them, even though we knew the euphoria we had experienced on that first day, decreased exponentially the longer we bore them.

Our bodies are amazing instruments; they are very good at adapting if given enough time, to the point where something that was annoying or even unbearable becomes normal and almost undetectable. I remember a few times on that hike where I would reach back over my shoulder just to make sure I was still carrying my pack. Now granted as the hike wore on and we ate more of the food that we carried, the packs did get lighter, but this lightening of the load was not so dramatic to offset the phenomenon of adaption taking place.

Throughout our lives, we all have been witnesses to this experience. Another example of this was when my parents and I lived in Johannesburg, South Africa. We lived in a suburb called Kempton Park. One of the features of this suburb was a large factory complex we had to drive past to get to our home. The factory manufactured a chemical that smelled incredibly bad. The first few months of passing this chemical plant would cause us to pinch our noses shut and gag, but after driving past this factory countless times, we ceased to smell the putrid stench. It was only when someone else was in the car with us would gag or grab their nose did we again become aware of the odor. The odor had not disappeared. We just became so accustomed to it, that it became part of our daily commute and therefore ceased to bother us.

One more example of this took place in the same Kempton Park neighborhood. Our home, though not close to the airport, was under the flight path that planes would take to land and take off at Jan Smuts International Airport, now called Oliver Tambo International Airport. When we first moved into our home the sound of the planes roaring over our heads every hour or so was annoying. After a few months of this, however, the roaring began to fade into the background of our consciousness. Our guests would have to remind us by their comments as they stared at our ceiling and pointed, "Wow, those planes are loud! Doesn't that bug you?"

Now don't get me wrong this adaption can be a good thing, but it does not only happen to us physically, or to our senses, it can do the most significant damage emotionally. For all of us carry emotional weight, burdens, that some of us have carried since our childhood. On many occasions, people might ask the same questions we were asked, "Wow that must be hard! Doesn't that bug you?"

Individuals, related groups of people, managerial teams, or even whole companies or organizations, can carry these emotional weights; no one is immune. These emotional weights have become part of us; we sleep, work, and conduct our daily lives with them, and never know that we are carrying something extra. Hints show up, but we do not recognize them or do not want to see the signs. Others might point them out, but we either ignore them or get angry with them for being insensitive or putting us on the spot. Therefore, we carry on with our daily rituals none the wiser that we carry something that is slowly eating away at us like cancer, sapping our energy and life force from us. We reluctantly shoulder our packs and continue our journey, telling ourselves, "This is just part of my life, something I need to bear." We ignore it hoping it will just go away. However, there is a problem with this philosophy because choosing to ignore a problem that does not make it disappear. All ignoring it does is hide it for a time while it grows like a fungus in a dark, damp place until it explodes. When that happens, it not only damages you but all who are within range of that explosion.

You see, it is our resistance to change, to release what we know must be released that prolongs our suffering and gets in the way of our eventual healing. We must keep getting out of our own way, and that can be difficult because our way is so familiar to us. It's been our way of life, even though it hasn't worked for us, it's very familiar. If we can give our past problems the much-needed attention they deserve, then we can move on. If we can add value to them instead of sweeping them under the rug, we can grow past the hurt and the pain that the past has dealt us. For us to do this, it's incredibly helpful to have a clear goal. If you have no goal, no vision, you're going to slip back into the way you have always done things. You will slip those packs back on your back and keep walking, just like you've always done. These goals, this vision needs to be pictured, and it needs to be specific. If you have been battling depression, cut out a picture of someone laughing, dancing, or enjoying life in some way. Pin it up and let that be the goal you aim to achieve.

We don't want to go back to familiar. The packs, though familiar, are draining our energy, our power and we need to have a method and a goal to get rid of them. We need a clear plan and vision to release us from the weights that are holding us back so that we can start grabbing our future with both hands. If one hand is on the rope of our past, it's a lot harder to grab hold (with commitment) to the rope of our future.

The ancient Roman Emperors were renowned for their ability to think up hideous forms of punishment. Most of us are familiar with the fact that crucifixion was one such form of punishment; however, there was another. In these ancient times, one of the brutal forms of punishment used for murders was to tie the dead body of the victim to the murder's back. The murderer would have to walk and live during every activity with this dead body tied to his or her back as a reminder of the committed crime. As the body decayed and rotted, it consumed, infected, and mutilated the living person who eventually died as a result. Though this is a graphic and disturbing picture, I need you to see that when you carry around unforgiveness, this is what happens to you. We don't even realize that we are carrying around the very object that can lead to our emotional and even physical demise and that if left long enough it will rot and decay within us.

CHAPTER TWO

Unpacking the Pack

"To be wronged is nothing unless you continue to remember it."
Confucius

So, what is this pack on our backs? What are these weights that we carry? All of us, no matter who we are, have experienced wounds in our lives. Four emotional weapons usually create these wounds:

1. What others have done to us.
2. What others have not done to us.
3. What others have said to us.
4. What others have not said to us.

I will go into more detail in a later chapter about each of these weapons. For now, I want to emphasize that these weapons are extremely effective in creating wounds that do not heal easily.

When you choose not to deal with a wound, it becomes infected, and finally, this infection can kill.

I think of the story of Karen Carpenter, who at a very young age encountered a deep wound from these emotional weapons, wielded by none other than her mother, Agnes. Karen's mom wielded the first weapon previously mentioned: *What others have not said to us.* The use of this weapon created a deep wound in Karen's life and eventually led to bulimia and death from a heart attack.

In his book *Little Girl Blue: The Life of Karen Carpenter* Randy Schmidt reveals the emotional problems at the core of Karen's eating disorder, which was her relationship with her mother (Agnes) and Agnes's inability to show the love and affection that Karen so desperately craved. Millions adored Karen, her circle of friends loved her dearly, but it was her mother's love she longed to receive. Although bulimia played a huge part in Karen Carpenter's death, her wound that was never properly dealt with was the ultimate cause.

It is amazing how even though we get used to these packs on our back, even though we do not even feel their presence any-more, their mere presence steals a little bit of our health, our emotions, our attitude and finally our purpose every day. For some of us, this siphoning of what I call the "Life Four" (playing off the words "Life Force") is minuscule. However, day after day this is happening, and just as the sun can drain a swimming pool of water one drop at a time, given enough time, your "Life Four" will become depleted. Unless you put a stop to the slow drain your health, emotions, attitude and purpose (HEAP) will suffer. We've all heard about being the top of the heap; well, when your "Life Four" becomes drained you land up at the bottom of the heap, worn out, confused and hurting. Certain factors come into play as to how fast your "Life Four" drains.

- The weight of the pack. (Severity of the wound.)
- How many packs you are carrying. (The number of wounds.)
- Is it your pack or someone else's? (Has someone else infected you or is it your wound?)
- How long you have been carrying the pack. (Spread of infection.)

Let's look at these factors briefly.

The Weight of the Pack

This factor has to do with the severity of the wound you have suffered. Some wounds are more severe than others. All wounds can cause damage if not dealt with; however, not all wounds are the same. A nasty word from a colleague at work does not create the same wound as a nasty word from our spouse or significant other. A boss's mistreatment will not carry the same weight as the mistreatment we receive from someone we love. All of these will create wounds. However, they do not share the same depth.

I would like to add here that all wounds left and not dealt with can become severe. If the colleague's nasty word is not handled, given time, its severity can be as deep as the nasty word was from your spouse. Certain wounds can drain us faster than others. As in the sun's example mentioned earlier, the sun has the power to drain a swimming pool of water, it doesn't happen as fast as a hole in the pool would, but the result is the same.

How Many Packs Are You Carrying?

This factor has a two-pronged effect. One, the more packs you are carrying, the more cumbersome the load. Second, the more packs you are carrying, the easier it is for you to pick up more. The more adept you are at picking up offenses, the more this makes you a professional offense hoarder. We see them all the time, people who are very quick to pick up a grudge and very unlikely to let it go.

In 1993, I decided to go on another hike. This one was in the Drakensberg Mountains in the province of KwaZulu-Natal, South Africa. The Drakensberg Mountains are the largest mountain range in South Africa and is considered one of the most treacherous. Thunderstorms with huge downpours can occur without warning causing flash flooding in dry riverbeds. Sudden snowstorms can spring up in the middle of summer, or rockslides with huge boulders can come crashing down hillsides without warning. These dangers do not change the fact that the mountains are breathtaking, and hiking trails litter the forested slopes.

The weekend before, I played a game of rugby and injured my shoulder. Since we made these hiking plans well in advance, I was not willing to call them off. My friends and I chose to hike one of the most dangerous of the trails. In fact, a week before that same trail claimed the life of another hiker. We were young, invincible, and foolish. Because of my shoulder injury, my pack was the lightest, and my friends carried the bulk of the load. We had many adventures on our short two-day hike, but one stands out to me when trying to explain the second factor in this draining of the "Life Four."

On the first day of the hike after being accosted by a troop of angry baboons, we wandered off our path and got lost. Armed with a compass and a map we decided to take a shortcut back to where we needed to be when suddenly we were confronted with a cliff blocking our path to where we wanted to go. Being adventurous or stupid—I think the latter probably describes us best—we decided to climb this sheer rock wall instead of turning back to go a long way around. The biggest problem was that my shoulder was in excruciating agony from carrying the lightest of packs. My best friend, Handre, decided to help me out by not only carrying his overloaded pack but mine as well. The ascent was perilous and slow. Halfway up my poor friend beside having to carry two packs had to help me as well by pushing me up some damp and slippery areas. Did I mention I was also afraid of heights?

I do not know how we managed to scale this cliff. We did succeed, barely, but a few truths can be learned from this experience. Namely, carrying One wound is bad enough, but many people are not just carrying one wound, they are carrying many. The more packs we carry, the quicker they drain us. Life can sometimes be an uphill, treacherous at times, slippery at others. How much more difficult are we making it when we are carrying these extra weights? Once my friend reached the top, he was exhausted and ready to call it quits. Is there any wonder that there are so many people calling it quits on life? Their packs have worn them out! They are carrying multiple overloaded packs, and they are draining them. These weights can make small hills feel like mountains.

Your Pack or Someone Else's?

This story also fits nicely with the third factor. If you were already carrying more than your fair share of packs, you would think you would not have room to carry more. Like my friend, though, others can share their packs with us if we are not careful. Suddenly we are carrying their weights as well which happens more often than we think, suddenly we are carrying other people's offenses, hurts, and disappointments. We take up their packs with glee and slowly our pools are draining like a sieve. Does this pack even belong to you?

Some years ago, I picked up an offense towards an individual whom I was working for at the time. I would go home every night and complain to my wife about the way this person was treating me. I complained that the person never listened to my ideas, didn't recognize my efforts, and broke promises after promise. This complaining, which was coming out of a wound, and might I add a wound that had nothing to do with this individual but one that I had carried since childhood, went on for a few months until I recognized what was going on. I was carrying a pack on my back that was affecting not only my relationship with this boss but also my relationship with my wife. I let it go. Almost a year later, the same boss invited my wife and me out for a meal. When I told my wife, her reply shocked me. "I don't want to go out with them!" she said vehemently. The poison in her reply surprised me. She hardly knew this man, had spent very little time with him, and when she had, he was kind and friendly to her.

What was the root of her bitterness? Then it hit me—this was not her pack! Even though almost a year earlier I had gotten rid of my pack, without knowing it I had passed it on to my wife. She had taken my wound on herself. When I let it go, I never told her, and for almost a year she had carried my pack on her shoulders, allowing it to weigh her down. This little episode taught me a valuable lesson: you can transfer wounds if you are not careful. You can pass them on to those you love, and now they too must carry a weight that is not theirs to carry in the first place.

How Long Have You Been Carrying the Pack?

The longer you have carried something, the greater the hold it has on you. In fact, you become more accustomed to the pack. In this case, older wounds have had longer to settle, to spread and to engrave themselves into your psyche. You have lived with them so long until they feel right; they feel like they belong. The wounds familiarity makes it tremendously difficult to get rid of them, not impossible just very difficult!

Swimming was one of my favorite exercises to keep fit. During one of my swim sessions I was messing around on a high dive board and by accident when diving off my foot scraped the rough edges of the board. During this period, I was also involved in long distance running and was becoming rather proud of myself for the miles I was able to run. This small scrape was an inconvenience, but not something to worry about. What I didn't know was that public swimming pools and diving boards have a lot of germs and my foot became infected. Here's the rub (no pun intended) I never dealt with the infection immediately. I under-estimated its severity until my foot became a swollen, infected mess.

No, I didn't lose my foot, but my running was adversely affected. The healing process was long, painful, and took over three months. When I was finally able to get back on the road, I had to start over because I lost all my previous progress. Discouragement set in and though I'm not proud to admit it I quit running. The effect of the infection was tremendous, and in this, a powerful principle is born. Infection always comes first, if not dealt with immediately the effect of this is a poison that starts to spread through our lives, draining us, sapping us of our "Life Four" until we are severely affected and crippled.

This book aims to help you let go of all the packs you are carrying. You must purge the deadly infection from your veins, restore the effectiveness of your "Life Four" and reverse the effect that this poison has had on your life in the present and into the future. I want to do it in small bites. I do not want to overwhelm you, but I know as we do this step by step the easier it becomes, and before long you will have realized that you have let go of all those packs that have been weighing you down! In that way, you can experience true freedom from those packs on your back!

CHAPTER THREE

Looking Under the Band-Aid

"What we avoid does not disappear, in fact when we turn around we find that it's been stalking us like a hungry tiger." Confucius

Band-Aids don't heal all they do is cover. When my daughters were younger every time they got hurt—be it a scratch, a cut, or even a slight scrape, they wanted Daddy to put on a Band-Aid. They did not care if Daddy first put on some ointment or cleaned the booboo; to them, it was all about the Band-Aid. This action seems to ring true for most of us when it comes to our emotional boo-boos. Most people who are wounded tend to run for a Band-Aid, bury the pain, cover the hurt up, do not talk about it, and pretend that it never happened. We avoid the pain instead of dealing with it, instead of rubbing on the right ointment that will facilitate the correct healing process. A band-aid is very good at covering and fulfilling the "out of sight out of mind!" attitude. We do this because dealing with pain is painful and we have a natural aversion to pain.

Here's the problem with boo-boos left unattended: they become infected and can eventually cripple. When I was in high school, our main sport was rugby. It was my school's religion, and anyone who considered themselves important played rugby. Dale College was an all-boys school, and it was an ego thing to be part of a rugby team. One of the seniors in our school never played rugby. Instead, he was a fantastic squash player (a type of racquetball with a smaller ball).

This young man was representing South Africa for squash and was one of the best in the country. In rugby, unlike football, there are only fifteen players in a team. At our school, we had ten senior teams for players who were in grades ten through twelve. These teams ranked from first team, which was the premier team, all the way down to the tenth team. In one of our high school derbies against one of our fiercest rival schools, the 10th team was short one player and our South African squash player was asked to step up and play. During the match, he took a hard knock to the knee and had to leave the field. I'm sure it was painful, but nothing was done about it. He never went for scans instead he just carried on ignoring the pain as just a bad bruise. What he did not know was that he had internal bleeding in his knee, which eventually turned gangrenous and our amazing squash player eventually lost his leg. This story illustrates a very serious point, when wounds are covered up they can cripple and even kill you.

It's important to know the severity of the wound. If our squash player had gone to someone who could have diagnosed the injury, he could have received the proper treatment and avoided losing his leg. We don't run to a doctor for every injury. Some injuries can be treated at home without expensive hospital bills. However, it would be a handy skill if we could have some way of diagnosing our wounds. For this to happen, we must look under the Band-Aids we have constructed. We must be willing to face the pain head-on.

When I was growing up my mom used to put a liquid called Mercurochrome on my cuts and scrapes. I hated that little red bottle! It stung like a thousand bees were assaulting you, though it did its job. My girls love the Band-Aids, but they hate the ointments and liquids I put on because they hurt. In today's world, the popular attitude is to avoid pain. Pain equals bad, and we must avoid it at all cost. People's Band-Aids can range from emotional withdrawal to alcohol and drug abuse to even suicide, the ultimate Band-Aid. All these options are for one reason only, to avoid pain, to not deal with it, to hide and bury it. Pain does not equal bad; it's the way our body and our emotions tell us that something is wrong. It's a warning system. And as we have seen, it's not dealing with what's under the Band-Aid that can have disastrous consequences.

Some wounds are more severe than others. You can usually tell how severe the wound is by using a simple pain scale. Using this scale, I will explain how we can diagnose the severity of our wounds.

This scale ranges from 0 to 10, 0 being no pain at all and 10 being the most severe pain that you can experience where you pass out due to pain and not blood loss. This scale is like the pain scale that doctors use to assess the type of pain you are experiencing. At level 5 the pain takes a turn from pain that is evident but not limiting daily life and activities to pain that affects life activities and emotional well-being. I need you to realize that these types of pain are real; it is what can and has happened to the human body. Let's look at this scale on the following page and then I will share with you how to utilize it to discern the wounds in your life.

Pain Scale

Pain Level	Description	Examples
0	No pain	
1	Pain is hardly noticeable.	Mosquito bite, Poison Ivy
2	Aware of pain when I pay attention to it.	An infected pimple, a pinch with a finger nail
3	Pain I can ignore but it bothers me.	An accidental cut, a punch to the nose, sunburn
4	Constantly aware of my pain but can continue with my activities.	Toothache, bee sting, stubbing your toe hard, 1st degree burn, bad sunburn
5	Think of my pain most of the time and it limits some activities.	Sprained ankle, lower back pain, 2nd degree burns
6	Think of my pain all the time. I give up on many activities.	A bad headache, several wasp stings, intense back pain
7	I am in pain all the time. The pain keeps me from doing most activities.	Average migraine headache, dislocated shoulder, root canal without anesthetic
8	My pain is so severe it's hard to think of anything else.	Child birth, intense migraine headache
9	My pain is all that I can think about. I can barely talk or move.	Throat cancer, deep lacerations, losing a finger, toe.
10	Can't think, speak or move due to pain.	Crushing injury, losing a large limb, like an arm or leg; skin flayed from body.

Imagine that I have a special ointment. This ointment has amazing properties. It can remove—with a blink of an eye—any pain that you are experiencing, no matter what the severity is and not only that but erase the event that caused that pain as if it never happened. Let me give you an example. Let us say that a wound you received was something someone said to you, for instance, a parent, or someone close to you. These words wounded you deeply, maybe this person said you were dumb or stupid or maybe he or she told you that you wouldn't amount to much. These harsh words can leave a deep wound in a child or even an adult. This wound like most emotional or physical wounds is painful. Now imagine for a second that I can use my special ointment. I can apply this ointment to the wound and not only will this ointment immediately take away the pain it will also erase the event that caused the pain as if it never happened.

The question I have for you is, "What would you be willing to pay me to use my special ointment?" I would like you to think now of something in your past that hurt you or created a wound in your life. Remember, this could fall into any one of the four categories mentioned earlier:

1. What people said to you.
2. What people didn't say to you.
3. What people did to you.
4. What people didn't do to you.

Once you have thought of this wound, write it down in the space provided in the "Actions to Freedom" section at the end of this chapter. Now, go back and look at the pain scale above and start at level 3: *Pain I can ignore, but it bothers me.* This type of pain is usually associated with a punch in the nose or sunburn or an accidental cut. There are two rules when using this pain chart:

- Be honest with yourself
- Do not exaggerate.

As you look at level 3 on the scale ask yourself, "Am I willing to experience the type of pain that a punch in the nose or an accidental cut can cause? Am I willing to live with that pain for as long as that type of injury lasts for this event, whatever it was, until it disappears as if it never happened?" If your answer is "yes," move up the scale until you get to a place where you decide that the necessary pain level would be too big a price to pay. When you get there go one step down and write down the level in the space provided next to the wound you received. Remember there are no right or wrong answers. It is entirely up to you to decide what you are willing to pay. Only you can judge the severity of the emotional wound you have endured. Some wounds will be very high on the scale and some very low. The higher the wound, the more severe it is and the more impact it will have on your life.

As we go through this book, I will first help you to get rid of the lower scaled wounds, as they are easier to handle, and will at least release some weight off you. All wounds have a pain level. The scale above determines the pain level, and that is the number you wrote next to your wound. You will release the lesser weights, to experience the joy of weight release. As you feel these little victories, I believe you will be spurred on to finally releasing those wounds that are the heaviest and most destructive.

I desire to help you let go of not just one or two of the packs you are carrying, but all of them. However, I want to do it in small bites. I do not want to overwhelm you, but I know as we do this step by step, the easier it becomes. And it won't be long before you let go of all those packs that have been weighing you down. What a joy when you suddenly realize that the past no longer has a hold on you, and when you look over your shoulder there is no longer a hungry tiger waiting to pounce. Now go ahead and think of another four wounds and do the same exercises mentioned above. Fill the wounds and pain levels in the spaces provided.

Actions to Freedom

Wound	Pain Level
1.	
2.	
3.	
4.	
5.	

CHAPTER FOUR

The Freedom of Choice

"Murder on many occasions has been due to an impulse of a moment of rage or blind anger, while the choice to refuse to forgive is a cold and deliberate act from the heart. Both steal life. However, which is worse, impulse or choice?"

Orrin Rudolph

"You are making me so angry!" Before the words left my mouth, I knew they were incorrect, yet I barreled on. "When Daddy tells you it is bedtime, I mean it's bedtime! Look at the time; it's already nine o'clock! You should have been in bed and asleep two hours ago!" and then again, "Sometimes you really frustrate me!"

My four-year-old, whose bedtime was at eight o'clock, was pushing her luck again, coming up with excuse after excuse to get me to come back into her bedroom. "I want a different music CD, my leg hurts, please go and find Elli, I can't sleep without Elli!" (even though her bed is overrun with a hundred other soft toys.)

And that was when I heard those incredibly incorrect words come out of my mouth. "You are making me so angry!"

For many of you, you might be asking, "Well? What's so wrong with that? She was making you angry, wasn't she?" Let us examine this statement. First, we have all heard these types of exclamations from, "That person is driving me crazy!" to "He is making me so angry!" or "She makes me so upset!" Though each of these exclamations sounds correct, they each have a huge fundamental flaw. No one can make you feel anything.

I know, right now, you might be saying, "Well, you just made me angry! How can you say that? People make you feel all the time! In fact, I've had people make me feel terrible!" Before you get angry with me, let me make my case, and then you can determine the validity of what I just told you.

Look at the diagram below. On the left side of the line is the events that happen to you, on the far right of the line are your emotions. In the middle is the word choice.

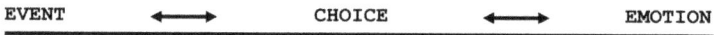

| EVENT | ⟷ | CHOICE | ⟷ | EMOTION |

Here is how this ECE principle works. An event happens to me. When that event takes place, a few factors come into play. The first thing that happens is the confrontation with choice: "Do I get mad? Do I stay calm?" etc. This choice happens within microseconds, so quickly, in fact, most times you are not even aware of it. Once the choice is made, the emotions follow. The formula that follows is a starting point to help you understand the power of choice. I call it the ABC's of Change through Choice.

$$A + B = C$$

The A in the formula stands for Acts. Acts are the situations, events, experiences and incidents that we face daily. These acts can be perpetrated by people or just be part of the world's operations. The B is for behavior. Our behaviors are actions we take to respond to the stimulus that we receive from the acts we experienced. The C equals the consequences of our actions and behaviors. They are the outcomes we reap because of the behaviors we sowed. So, the formula plays out as such: The acts of others, the events, and experiences that we face, *plus* the way we behave in our responses to these stimuli, *equals* the consequences reaped in our lives.

Let me ask you this question. Of the above formula, what part are you responsible for? If you answered, "my behaviors," then you are correct. The only part of the formula that you are responsible for is the behavior you choose as a response to the acts that happened to you. You have no control over these acts. Things happen that you cannot control. Stuff happens that is not planned. You do not get out of bed in the morning knowing what's going to happen every minute of your day. The only thing you can control is your behaviors by which you respond to these experiences.

I would now like to add an extra sum to this formula.

$$A + (Space) + B = C$$

The A still stands for the Acts; the B equals Behaviors, however between the A and the B a small space exists, in this space rests our choices. Now, these choices are affected by another element, and we call this Habit.

I have added a plus and minus sign between habit and choice. Your choices are affected by your habits. The stronger the habit is in that area the more it subtracts from the size of your choice. In other words, if you are used to reacting in a certain way repeatedly then when you have an opportunity to react in that way again, you will. Here's the reason why: because you have now developed a habit in that area of reaction, it almost feels like you have no choice, you merely react.

Constant repetition of any behavior over a period creates a habit. That period can be anywhere from eighteen to two hundred and fifty-four days. A cliché says, "Practice makes perfect." Although many clichés are true, this one is false. Practice does not make perfect because no human is perfect. What practice does is it makes permanent. Through our repeated behaviors and responses, we are, in fact, practicing and we aren't consciously aware of it. The repetition of this behavior becomes a set pattern in our lives that is very hard to break. What's more, it occurs, seemingly, without thought or planning. What we are doing in affect, is reprogramming our minds. We are reprogramming it to blaze a new path, one that might never have existed before. The C which once stood for consequence now turns into change, and this change affects our consequences.

For example, people who react negatively to bad driving habits do not think they have any choice but to react the way they do. They shout and scream and show rude signs to fellow drivers who might have cut them off or exhibited a bad-driving habit of their own. When these events occur, rude drivers still have the choice to react calmly. However, because they have repetitively reacted a certain way, when the act occurs their reaction almost seems instantaneous, and their choices head down a well-beaten path. The choice that they have to react differently is now so small that it is practically non-existent. We have seen the consequences of these drivers when they don't allow their choices to effect change, and so many times, those consequences are not pretty! I've seen a simple rude sign turn into road rage. The good news is that even though the choice they have to react differently is small if worked on it can increase in size.

Our home is on a lake, and I love to go fishing. There is a large lot next to ours that does not have a home on at present. Because of that, especially in summer, the lot looks like a jungle, especially close to the water's edge. Did I mention I love to fish? Some of the best fishing spots are on that lot, and to get to them I have to do, as we say in South Africa a lot of Bundu Bashing (bushwhacking). At first, getting to those great fishing spots was difficult because of the overgrowth. But over time, the more I headed to my favorite fishing spot (sometimes twice a day) I started wearing a well-trodden path. By the end of summer, I had no difficulty getting to the various fishing spots. In the same way, the more you practice choice, the path of your new behavior will grow easier for you to identify and broader for you to walk. Something else happens too. The old path your behaviors would take you down start to become overgrown from lack of use, and your mind will stop paying attention to it, mainly because it can't see the old path anymore. All it sees now is the new one.

At the beginning of this chapter, I made a statement that no one can make you feel the way you do, that you have a choice. If we can grasp this concept, it will liberate us from the bondage of making poor choices. When I tell my children that they are making me angry or frustrating me, what I am really telling them is that they have power over my emotions. If they have power over my emotions, then others will subsequently have power over their emotions. We must learn that real freedom of choice is that you are stopping the cycle of giving others your power and allowing others to take your power.

I will revisit this concept of choice in a later chapter, but for now, it is tremendously important that we begin to assimilate this concept into our lives. If we cannot, we will not be able to let things go effectively.

CHAPTER FIVE

❀

The Elephant in the Room

"We must develop and maintain the capacity to forgive. He who is devoid of the power to forgive is devoid of the power to love. There is some good in the worst of us and some evil in the best of us. When we discover this, we are less prone to hate our enemies."
Rev. Dr. Martin Luther King, Jr.

Habits . . . we all have them. They are the actions and behaviors we exhibit that happen seemingly without our consent. To understand habits, we need to examine the human mind. Most people accept that the human mind is made up of two parts: the conscious mind also known as the neocortex, and the subconscious mind or the limbic system. I will explain these two parts by using two illustrations.

The first illustration is that of an iceberg. We will label the part of the iceberg above the water the conscious mind, and the larger part found beneath the water the subconscious mind. The subconscious mind is the larger part of us. It is the invisible part where we store everything; is also the part we sometimes try to hide. This invisible bulk called our subconscious mind controls everything from brushing our teeth, getting dressed in the morning, driving our cars to and from work, to what foods we enjoy.

We can also imagine the subconscious part of our mind as an Indian elephant. We have all seen pictures or films of these elephants and their riders. These majestic animals do amazing tasks seemingly controlled by a mere flick of a stick from the diminutive rider perched on its back. This animal has incredible power; it can lift trees with its trunk, push boulders, and clear paths in the jungle. The elephant can easily cast the rider off its back but does not. So how can this human control this elephant? The elephant does what it is conditioned to do. It does what the rider has taught it to do. Our subconscious minds work the same way. Which brings us to the purpose of the conscious mind, and that is to help us learn new things.

When we are confronted with additional information, it must pass through the top part of the iceberg (the conscious mind). Our conscious mind will either throw this information away or retain it. If the elephant is to learn new commands or tasks, the rider will have to teach it. The rider needs to understand that this latest information or behavior is correct and beneficial for the elephant to learn before the rider will attempt to teach the new behavior to the elephant; this is no easy task. As we know elephants, like mules can sometimes be stubborn, and so can our subconscious mind, when confronted with new information or behavior. Like the stubborn elephant, our subconscious mind wants to do what it has been doing. It wants to take whatever path it has been taking and exhibit whatever behavior it has been exhibiting. So, when the rider tries to instill a new path or a new behavior, the elephant will feel that this information is wrong, and it will fight against it. That is why it is critical that the rider has already chosen to teach the new information. If the rider has not reached a conscious decision that this new information is beneficial but still attempts to teach it to the elephant anyway, the elephant will win.

When I moved from South Africa to the United States, one of the first things that I needed to relearn was how to drive a car. Even though I had been driving a car for many years back in South Africa, we drove on the left-hand side of the road. I was dreading the move from driving on the left to driving on the right. When I first climbed into the vehicle, I prepared my conscious. I had come to a conscious decision that learning to ride on the right side of the road was very beneficial for me. I had also chosen to go through the process of learning this new driving behavior. As expected when I got into the car, the steering wheel was on the left-hand side of the car, not the right, and the gearshift was on my right side, not the left. The only thing that was familiar was the orientation of the brakes, clutch, and gas pedals. Even though I had mentally prepared for the differences, made my choices and accepted the benefits, when I got into the car a little voice inside my head was telling me that this was wrong. My elephant did not want anything to do with this new driving method because in its mind this was wrong. It was not what it had been doing for the last twelve years; it liked the old way of doing things, and it did not want to change. This behavior from my elephant subsequently affected my feelings. As I sat in the driver's seat, my feelings told me that this was all wrong. When I got out onto the road that little voice started screaming, "*You are on the wrong side of the road!*" If someone had asked me that day, "Are you driving correctly?" I would have told them yes. Because my rider had gone through the process of decision, he knew this was right. But if someone had asked me that day, "Do you feel like you are driving correctly?" I would have replied emphatically, "No, this feels wrong!" I do know one thing that if I listened to my elephant, I would have been in serious trouble. Driving on the wrong side of the road could have had dire consequences!

The elephant aids the rider in choices by telling him that anything different or new is wrong. Its most powerful weapon used against the rider is his very own feelings. We have been taught from very young to listen to our feelings. When our feelings tell us something, we tend to listen and obey. These feelings are always and only created by our elephant's perceptions. In my case, the elephant perceived that riding on the left-hand side of the road was correct and that anything else was wrong and dangerous. He learned this through 12 years of repetition, and if not challenged would stay that way until he died.

A woman has a husband who continuously mistreats her. He treats her like a slave at times. Every morning at five he kicks her out of bed and tells her to make his breakfast and coffee. He tells her that she is dumb, stupid and no good. This behavior goes on year after year until one day he dies. She is free from the abuse. A few years later she meets another man, and eventually, they get married. This man is kind and loving. He has nothing but good intentions towards her. On the first morning of their honeymoon, he asks her politely if she would make him some coffee. Immediately feelings of resentment and anger spring up. Where did these feelings come from? Did they come from the event, which was him asking her for some coffee? No! Did this man cause her to feel angry and resentful? No! These feelings of anger and resentment came from her perception or her interpretation of the event. How she felt correlated directly with her old husband's behavior that was repeated so often in her life until her belief became cemented. She now believed that when a man asked her to do something, it was not a suggestion but rather a command. And this incorrect interpretation or perception solicited a reaction within her; this reaction created the emotions. Interpretations of events are a powerful stimulus of emotions that then ultimately lead to behavior.

A pastor friend told me a story of a man he was counseling. This man (let's call him Mike) had a history of bad relationships and was having serious marital problems with his wife, leading to a possible divorce. In fact, Mike was having problems with his mother whom he hated, his wife, and every other woman in his life.

Mike's main problem was his reaction to confrontation. If a woman said anything to him that came across in any way as accusatory, he would explode. He usually overreacted. In other words, his reaction never fit the experience. He told my friend that when his wife said anything to him, from the time it took to come out of her mouth and register in his brain, it would be distorted. Mike said that he had a problem with distorted perception, "My wife would say something to me, and I would hear her judging me, or checking up on me, or something negative," These overreactions had caused considerable damage to his marriage and to every relationship Mike ever had with a woman.

My friend and Mike revisited his childhood, where a very interesting experience surfaced. During his childhood, Mike lived in Louisiana near Lake Pontchartrain. His dad had taken Mike, who then was four years old and his three-year-old brother to visit friends across the lake. During the visit, Mike's father was visiting with his friends inside the home. Mike and his brother were playing in the backyard where there happened to be an un-fenced pool. He took his eyes off his brother for a second and his brother tripped and plunged into the deep swimming pool. Mike did not know what to do so he ran back into the house to alert his father. His dad rushed down to the pool, dived in and pulled Mike's brother out, then using mouth to mouth, he resuscitated his son. They wrapped up Mike's brother in a warm blanket and drove home. When they finally arrived home and pulled the car up to the back door of the house, Mike's mom met them. She was beside herself, shouting and making accusations out of fear and anxiety. During this tirade, Mike's mom made this statement: "He couldn't have fallen in on his own!" and a four-year-old little boy heard his mother saying, "You pushed him!"

From that moment on a deep root of anger and bitterness was planted in Mike's heart. As Mike grew older, his anger and bitterness led to a deep relational dysfunction with his mother, eventually his wife and then every other woman in his life. What Mike finally came to realize was that his mom was not speaking to him, but rather she was directing her anger towards his father. What Mike realized was that what she was saying to his dad was, "If you were watching him he would not have fallen into the pool!" It had nothing to do with Mike. But he misheard, and a wound was created that infected his life from that point on. An incorrect interpretation of an event that occurred when he was a child helped to form Mike's distorted perception of women. And we all know that children are bad interpreters, yet nevertheless, they interpret events just the same.

When an event or experience occurs, we are presented with a choice of how to interpret this event. The interpretation that we come up with can be true or false. Our interpretation becomes our truth. This interpretation—a filter, if you will—creates a perception by which all future events and experiences will be interpreted. This perception creates an internal reaction that generates emotions within us. These emotions are very real but most often produced by an erroneous perception. And these emotions play a huge part in the way we behave, react and respond. The more we react and respond in the same way is ultimately continuous practice which creates habits. Depending on how we choose to act on these emotions will either create a positive or negative behavior that then determines the outcome of the situation. It is important to note that we are never left without choice throughout this entire process. No matter how bad the learned behavior was (Habit), we still have a choice.

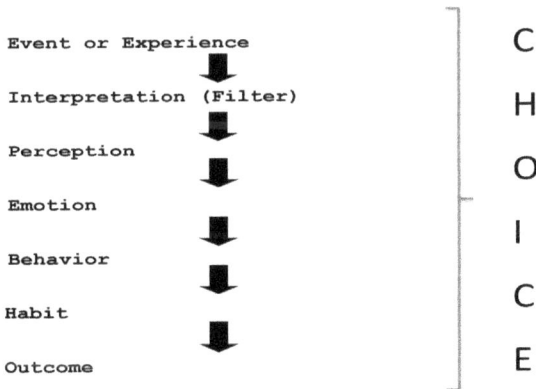

Event or Experience

Interpretation (Filter)

Perception

Emotion

Behavior

Habit

Outcome

C
H
O
I
C
E

Actions to Freedom

Use the chart on the next page. Think of embarrassing behavior that you have in your life. This behavior raises its ugly head repeatedly especially when certain events happen. And when these events happen, you always respond to the situation in the same way. Once you have thought of this behavior, write it in the following chart. I have filled in the chart on the left, as an example. The perception will be your hardest part to fill in. When filling in the perception, close your eyes and imagine yourself in the situation. Feel the emotions and see your behavior.

Once you have done that, ask yourself what that little voice is telling you. I know that it's telling you something because if it weren't, you wouldn't be acting the way you are. Remember the little voice you are hearing is coming from your interpretation. If you look at my perception, you see that it is not rational. How could I even think that I am a loser if my team is losing? How does that even make sense? You start to realize that your perceptions are produced because everything you experience goes through your interpretation filter.

Some of us have heard the saying, "Looking at the world through rose-colored spectacles." Sometimes our spectacles are not rose covered rather they are covered in something that might smell as sweet as a rose. Our interpretation of events can color the rest of our lives. This filter produces perceptions that are near impossible to change unless we deal with it. We must dig up the root of the tree that has produced the poison fruit.

Example	Experience
Event/Experience: I lose a game, or my team loses a game	Event/Experience:
Interpretation: Losing is only for losers!	Interpretation:
Perception: If I'm losing or my team is losing, I'm a loser!	Perception:
Emotion: Anger, frustration	Emotion:
Behavior: Shouting, cursing	Behavior:
Outcome: Embarrassment, guilt	Outcome:

Part Two:

The Road to Bitterness

CHAPTER SIX

Sticks and Stones

"That's what careless words do. They make people love you a little less." Arundhati Roy, The God of Small Things

"Sticks and stones will break my bones, but words will never harm me!" Parents have taught their children this rhyme for many years, but just like many other things that we have taught our kids that sound sweet and nice this rhyme is a dangerous philosophy. Now I know why we want our kids to say this when someone says something nasty to them. We want to protect them from the hurt of teasing and nasty words. The problem is that this rhyme teaches our children two incorrect ways of thinking. First, words do not harm, and second, if words do not harm, then people can say whatever they want.

Misused words can be the most devastating weapons used against someone. Those who have broken their bones know it immediately and seek help for healing. While bones can heal after a period, misused words are subtler in their process of creating injury. People can carry these wounds for years or even until they die without knowing the devastation these words have caused.

In the first chapter, I told you about four weapons that create wounds. In this chapter, we will discuss two of these weapons. We will also look at the types of wounds these weapons create and why they are so devastating to someone.

What People Say to Us (Sniper Rifle)

The first of these weapons is the weapon of *What people say to us.* This weapon has been responsible for some of the deepest wounds in peoples' lives. I refer to this weapon as the *sniper rifle* because words spoken in jest or seriousness tend to go straight to our hearts, just like a sniper's bullet would. A sniper always aims at the heart; this is known as a kill shot because it will kill you one hundred percent of the time. Has anyone ever said something to you that immediately hurt you or gave you the feeling that you had been punched in the gut? I am sure this has happened to all of us. Why that strong feeling? Why the sudden pain? Because words have this *sniper rifle* effect and they shoot straight to the heart.

As I said, I grew up in beautiful South Africa. My childhood was amazing, living under the African skies; although my early home life at times was difficult. My father was ex-military, and he grew up in a tough home with seven brothers and sisters vying for their parent's affection. Dad's mom was a hard woman who expected a lot from her children especially her two eldest sons. My father's dad was an alcoholic who never knew how to give affection. These were my father's role models. Looking back all these years later, I now understand why my upbringing was filled with *sniper rifle* statements and, as you will learn later in this chapter, *time bombs*.

One of the sniper bullets I want to focus on in my life was the word "stupid," which was uttered numerous times from my dad's mouth in my early days of growing up. "Orrin, why are you so stupid?" and "That was so stupid. Or "What's wrong with you, are you stupid or something?" Stupid, dumb, idiot, all these words and more are bullets that head straight to the heart and can cause insurmountable damage. I remember watching one of my favorite movie characters, James Bond in *The World is Not Enough*. An assassin shot the main villain in the head. The bullet slowly worked its way through his brain until the prognosis was that he would eventually die. But before he died, he had to deal with one of the side effects which was being impervious to pain. In other words, he felt nothing!

Have you ever wondered why someone you know seems to be impervious to the way they treat others? They seem to feel no remorse for either what they say or what others say about them; this is a side effect of too many bullets to the heart. If not dealt with these bullets will work their way deeper into the person's heart and finally kill off their emotions entirely.

I remember one day after one of my dad's tirades, when I stood in front of the mirror in my bedroom, at eleven years old and told myself, "Orrin, you are stupid. You are dumb. You are an idiot. You will become nothing!" When your inner voice starts agreeing with the outer voices, you know the sniper bullet has found its target—the heart. An almost immediate effect of the mirror incident was that my grades at school took a huge dip. I was beginning to believe the words my dad had spoken to me. And this belief was having a dire effect on my life. My motivation in schoolwork took a drastic plunge, and I began questioning my abilities. A wound had taken place, and it began to work inward, going deeper into my heart.

What are the things that people have said to you? Words may not be able to break bones, but as for harming you, they can create some of the most devastating wounds. Most of these wounds begin early and parents, teachers, friends or other children can inflict them. The wounds carry on into adult life and are many times echoed by spouses, bosses and work colleagues. Until we surgically remove the sniper bullets, they will continue to work inward killing off our emotions and creating a wound that can be fatal.

What Others Don't Say (Time Bomb)

Let us talk about the second weapon. This weapon, *What others don't say* I will call a *time bomb.* What is this weapon? As I shared in an earlier story about Karen Carpenter, one of the wounds Karen picked up was this time bomb wound. She never felt that her mom loved her because her mom rarely told her. I experienced the same type of time bomb in my early childhood. Because my dad had not ever received that type of affirmation from his parents, he didn't know how to pass it on to me. While I was growing up, I very rarely, if ever, heard my dad say, "Son, I love you." Unspoken words can be just as devastating as spoken words. We don't know the depth of devastation until the lack of these words starts to create behavior in us that can harm others and us.

So why do I call it the time bomb? Everyone has a deep need to feel loved and appreciated by others. When this need goes unmet, a timer is set off in us. The timer counts down until an explosion takes place. There are three main types of explosions:

1. An explosion of self-loathing.
2. An explosion of overcompensating.
3. An explosion of damaging behavior.

An Explosion of Self-Loathing

An explosion of self-loathing is expressed many times by the behavior we aim at ourselves. It is anger turned inwards. Instead of our anger turned towards those that have harmed us we aim our anger at ourselves. And in turn, we use our behavior to harm ourselves. The more recognizable behaviors are Anorexia, Bulimia, self-mutilation, and depression. While it is true that some depression can be chemical or hormonal imbalance etc., I believe that a large percentage of depression originates from this time-bomb. The ultimate behavior in this inward hatred is suicide. Suicide is a permanent solution to a temporary problem. It is the ultimate expression of anger turned inward.

An Explosion of Overcompensating

An explosion of overcompensating is expressed through behavior aimed outward or upward. Like a flare shot into the night, these explosive actions are aimed to draw attention our way. We seek ways to satisfy our deep need for appreciation and love. One of the subconscious ways we try and do this is to gain the approval or sympathy of others. My time bomb explosion went off in my teen years. Now, you might say, "Orrin, all teens are looking for attention!" That might be true. However, this type of explosion is much more evident and damaging. In order to illustrate this point, I will strip myself bare to reveal the lengths people will go to get this attention.

When I was seventeen, I was very involved in the youth group in the church my parents attended. At the end of each year, youth groups across South Africa would journey up to a beautiful campsite in South Africa's northern province known as the Transvaal. We would head there by bus, and the journey would take about twelve hours. The event was known as "Youth Week," and would play host to about fifteen hundred young people. On this particular week, I was fascinated with a young lady in my youth group. I was desperate for her attention. In retrospect, I believe what I did next was not only for this young lady's benefit but also for anyone else willing to give me the attention I craved. During that week I faked passing out! That's right, you read correctly.

The first time I faked passing out was during a soccer game, where I was the goalie. Advantageously the ball smacked me on the side of the head. I was fine, but that young lady was on the sidelines watching so I faked a concussion! To my amazement as I lay there I got what I wanted—hers and a lot of others attention and sympathy. In my mind, it worked.

How far did I push this charade? Far enough during that week to receive a saline drip. Yes, I allowed people to stick needles in my arms, just to get my need for attention met. I told you I was about to strip myself bare. As I look back now this and many episodes in my life are an embarrassment. But I want to show you how far people are willing to go to get attention.

Many others have gone further than I did to get attention because this explosion drives people to behave irrationally. Just because you have not done something as crazy as I did, does not mean that this explosion is not working in you. Sometimes this attention-getting behavior can be very subtle, as it became later in my life. It turned into the behavior of me always trying to prove myself to others. Through either subtle bragging or being the ultimate diplomat, I was trying to get everyone to like me. It was a need for approval from others so that I could get along with others no matter what that meant.

An Exposition of Damaging Behavior

An explosion of damaging behavior is anger turned outward. "Going Postal" is a term derived from a series of incidents from 1983 onward in which United States Postal Service (USPS) workers shot and killed managers, fellow workers, and members of the police or general public in acts of mass murder. Between 1986 and 1997, more than 40 people were gunned down by spree killers in at least 20 incidents of workplace rage.

We live in an angry society. All we need to do is turn on the news, and we see explosions almost daily. Some of the most recent events are 1999's Columbine, 2006's Amish Schoolhouse shooting, 2007's Virginia Tech, 2012's Colorado Theatre massacre and Sandy Hook Elementary shootings, and finally, the 2018 high school massacre which took place in Parkland, Florida. All these examples are extreme, yet as we learned in an earlier chapter if left unchecked, these wounds can have dramatic and devastating results.

Let's take a look at some less extreme examples. Why do some people have such a short temper, or cry at the slightest hint of offense? Why is it that some people do not need much to explode into violence or others into shouting tirades? Still, others who become so frustrated that they punch walls or scream and cuss at themselves and others.

These explosions, like Mount St. Helens needed time to build. The moment these hurts are received, the time bomb is planted, and the clock begins to tick. Some take longer than others, but one thing is for sure unless deactivated there will be an explosion. And depending on the size and amount of the bombs will determine the size, severity, and regularity of the explosions.

CHAPTER SEVEN

Action Speaks Louder Than Words

"No snowflake in an avalanche ever feels responsible." Voltaire

As we have discovered words are incredibly powerful, but what we do can speak much louder than our words. The next two weapons are all about our actions and the profound effect they can have on our lives. Many children have watched as their parents have told them one thing yet in the very next second done the opposite. As a father, I know the difficulty of keeping my words and actions congruent. There is a saying, "Monkey see, monkey do." I've been on both sides of the monkey; I've been the monkey that does and the one that taught the monkey their actions. The question is, who is the bigger monkey?

Children are like mirrors; they reflect what is in front of them. I had this truth hammered home recently. I had lost my temper with my oldest daughter. An old habit, I will discuss later, had surfaced. I raised my voice at her and let my temper get the better of me. Of course, I felt guilty about the way I behaved and apologized to her for my actions. Two hours later I heard her do the very same thing that I had done to her a few hours earlier to her younger sister. I had to confront her and deal with her temper. It reminded me that all she was doing was what I had taught her throughout her younger years. Let's look at the first of the action weapons.

What People Do to Us (Garrote)

What people do to us is the first of the action weapons. This weapon is a lot more visible than the second as we can see these actions occurring. We will refer to this weapon as the *garrote*. Potentially, the actions of others can violently choke you to death! Have you ever had anyone do something to you that seemed to take your breath away—and not in a good way? Their actions have such a profound effect that it feels like they have sucked out all the oxygen in the room. Other people's actions can have this devastating effect.

The effect of losing your breath is most profound the very first time a person does something to you. These four examples will help you understand what I mean.

- A woman whose boyfriend or husband hits her the first time is devastated.
- A person who catches someone close to them in a lie for the first time cannot believe it happened.

- A child who experiences the person they trust the most sexually abuse them the first time cannot comprehend why this person would violate them.
- A spouse catching their significant other in an affair is in disbelief that such a thing could happen.

The very first time is always the most painful as it comes as a surprise and steals your breath away. You weren't expecting it because many times these people are the people you trusted, people who could have told you many times that they loved you. There is an almost immediate draining of the "Life Four," and the pain can almost be unbearable.

One of the posts a friend of mine made on Facebook the other day caught my attention. He asked a simple question. "Why is that the people who you love the most, hurt you the most?" The answer is in the question, and it is this: "The people you love the most." The closer you are to someone the more open, the more vulnerable you are; therefore, your defenses are down, you are not expecting them to attack you, harm you, lie to you, or abuse you. And when they do it's like a punch from behind that inflicts a severe wound.

Once again, I will expose an embarrassment from my past to illustrate this point. When I was ten years old, a new family member arrived, a beautiful bouncing baby girl, my sister. I had grown up until then as mostly an only child. I say "mostly" as I did have a younger brother; however, my brother was severely handicapped and restricted to a stroller. He was a nine-year-old trapped in a one-year-old's body, so I was the king of the roost. Between the age difference and the resentment, I felt I was no longer the only child, so my sister and I never had the best of relationships growing up.

I remember a specific event that had occurred between the two of us. While I do not remember the cause, I do remember the result. I was in my senior year and my beautiful sister, ten years my junior who must have been eight years old had done something. The mere fact I can't remember what she had done shows just how insignificant it was and how little it took for me to lose my temper. I exploded, chased her down, grabbed her by her little shoulders, lifted her up and pinned her to the wall while screaming at her. One thing haunted me for a long time whenever I recalled that event. I remember vividly the look in my baby sister's eyes: surprise, fear, confusion, disappointment and most of all deep hurt. I could almost hear her eyes sending me a message, "You're my brother, and I love you, why are you doing this to me?"

Fast-forward years later while sitting down with my same beautiful sister I came to discover that this experience had a profound effect on her. My sister did not remember the words, but she did remember the way I grabbed her, the way I lifted her up and shoved her against the wall. Those actions scarred and devastated her, resulting in our strained adult relationship years later. Her brother in those few actions had shown her more than any words could have. They had told her that I hated her and that she was in my way. Now I could deny those allegations, but why bother because she was right. I love my sister, but in the same way, I was jealous of her. She was daddy's little girl, and Dad loved her. She got something from him that I so deeply wanted—his love and affection. I never felt my dad loved me, but I knew he loved her and this insane jealousy made me hate her; she was in the way of me getting Dad's love.

This action had stolen the breath from my sister. There was always that uncomfortable underlying atmosphere when we were together. While we were always polite to one another, our relationship was non-existent.

Our actions can have long-standing consequences. The sad thing is that those that commit these actions can move on and forget what they have done, but the recipients of the *garrote* do not forget the experience of the sensation of their breath being taken away. The scars are still etched around their emotional throats and burned into their minds. From that moment on, the pain of the garrote can steal the very essence of the way they live their lives.

What People Don't Do (Poison)

What people don't do can also have a long-lasting effect. All of us have had people do things to us that have hurt us. These actions are not hard to identify in our lives, but other actions are far less detectable but just as deadly. We will call this weapon, *poison.*

As we know, poison can kill instantly. As an avid watcher of crime shows, I have come to realize that one of the features of those who poison others is that they do it in small doses so that their crimes will go undetected. Their victims are slowly poisoned over a period until finally, they succumb to the deadly cocktail. So, what do people not do? They do not follow through on their promises. Has anyone ever broken a promise that they made to you? How did that make you feel? How did that affect the trust you had for that person? The size of the promise broken, just like the amount of poison ingested, can have a tremendous effect on the wound it causes and the resulting symptoms.

A young woman I had been counseling, we will call her Michelle, had been battling with a serious trust issue. According to Michelle, her husband was always lying and cheating on her. Besides her husband, others were always deceiving her. People were not to be trusted. The sad thing was that all this was in her mind. Her husband was faithful, her friends were trustworthy, and the only common denominator was one person, Michelle. So, what happened to cause her not to trust anyone? In her own words, "I want to trust people, but I just can't. I know they are going to let me down!"

So, did she come out of a past relationship where a spouse or significant other had deceived her? No. Did friends lie to her in her past? No. So what happened? When Michelle was ten years old, her dad promised to buy her a beautiful new bicycle. She had been dreaming of owning this bicycle. The only condition was she would receive this bicycle if she achieved all A's on her final report card. Now, this was not just any bicycle. It had gears and decals and all the bells and whistles that a little girl could ever imagine. Michelle cut the picture of the bicycle out of a catalog and pinned it up in a prominent position next to her bed. Every night she would gaze longingly at the picture before she went to bed.

Finally, the school year ended, and her report card arrived. Michelle got all A's. She was finally going to realize her dream; the bicycle would soon be hers. What Michelle did not know was that her dad's business had experienced financial difficulties all year which forced him to close it and declare bankruptcy. Because of these unfortunate circumstances and even more pressing family obligations, he did not get the bicycle for Michelle as promised. Talk of bankruptcy, family priorities, financial considerations, and more promises that when the family's financial situation was better, they would buy the bicycle, were just words to a ten-year-old girl who had longed for this bicycle for more than a year. They fell on deaf ears, and all she could see was her dream going up in flames because of a broken promise. There was no bicycle, a bicycle she had dreamed of, a bicycle that she had worked hard for, but most importantly a bicycle that she had been promised.

Broken Promises

Broken promises, the arsenic of emotional poison can be as deadly as the real-life poison to a person's emotions, and just like the real poison, the dosage amount determines the damage it causes.

For Michelle, the broken promise when she was ten had been a huge emotional blow. So, what determines the size of the dose? Two determinants play a part in how big a dose of this poison we ingest: trust and expectations.

Trust

The type of trust relationship we have with the person who makes the promise has a large part to play in how open we are to receive the dose. The amount of trust between you and that person decides whether you are immune or wide open to being severely poisoned by their broken promises. I want to interject here that immunity is not necessarily a good thing. For you to build immunity, you must ingest small doses of poison over time. Eventually, your emotions become seared towards the person in question which is not healthy nor to be desired. Dr. Frank Crane says it best, "You may be deceived if you trust too much, but you will live in torment if you don't trust enough."

I will admit that at times I have a hard time trusting certain people. I have grown immune to their promises. I develop my feelings of distrust after someone has done something intentionally or unintentionally that makes me question their character. They have told me one thing and done another. They promise me the beach and deliver a grain of sand. Let's be honest. If you're in any relationship with someone long enough, from time to time, they're going to act in a way that will bring the trust issue to the forefront. We all have a trust meter like the diagram that follows.

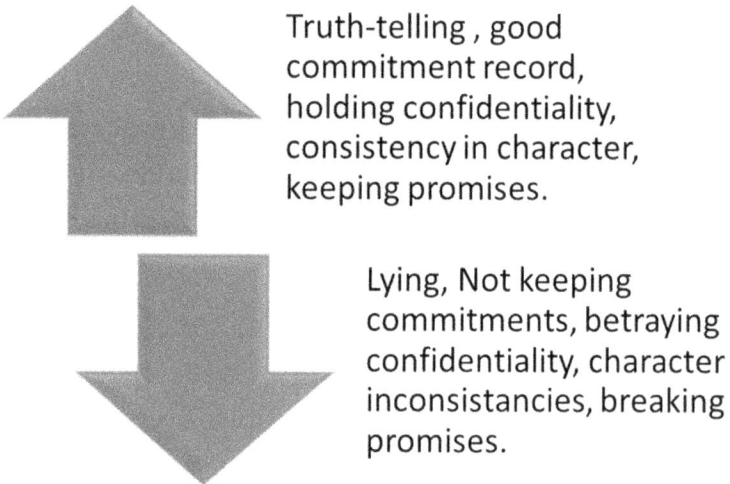

Truth-telling , good commitment record, holding confidentiality, consistency in character, keeping promises.

Lying, Not keeping commitments, betraying confidentiality, character inconsistancies, breaking promises.

Every time you interact with another person your trust meter goes up or down based on at least five factors.

- The person's truth-telling record
- The person's commitment-keeping pattern
- The person's ability to keep matters confidential
- The person's consistency in character
- The person's track record of keeping the promises they make

These factors are indicators in all your relationships. As a ten-year-old, Michelle's trust meter towards her father was high, the little gauge was pointing close to full, but I would guess that if you looked at that little pointer after the promise was broken it would have been pointing close to empty.

Now some of you need to realize your trust meter is broken. It's giving you false readings. Because of the baggage from your past, your trust meter is malfunctioning. Just like Michelle's was when I was counseling her; the indicator gauge was stuck on empty. It didn't matter anymore the type of relationship she was involved in, it remained on empty and unlike healthy trust meters was not allowed to fill up.

Expectations

The second determinant is our expectations, our expectations of the people that made the promises, but even more critical the expectations of the promise itself.

For Michelle the promise was huge. In her mind, she was already riding the bike and showing it off to her friends. Her mind was already making plans; for her the bicycle was a foregone conclusion. When the promise of the bicycle was not delivered upon, it was no longer about the promise for Michelle but all that she was expecting the promise to deliver. Her little world was tied up in the dream of what the promise her dad made was going to deliver. Our expectations set us up for disappointment, especially when our expectations are rigid and unyielding. Therefore, any variance from what we expect will disappoint us because we have not allowed any room for error. We have not based our expectations on the reality that very rarely do we get everything we are expecting. However, that does not stop us from expecting, nor should it. Rather we should temper our expectations by cultivating the soil of our hearts—our self-esteem, which we will discuss in a later chapter. If not, the higher our expectations are, the greater the disappointment we will experience because our very self is tied up in the result.

Expectations vs. Disappointments

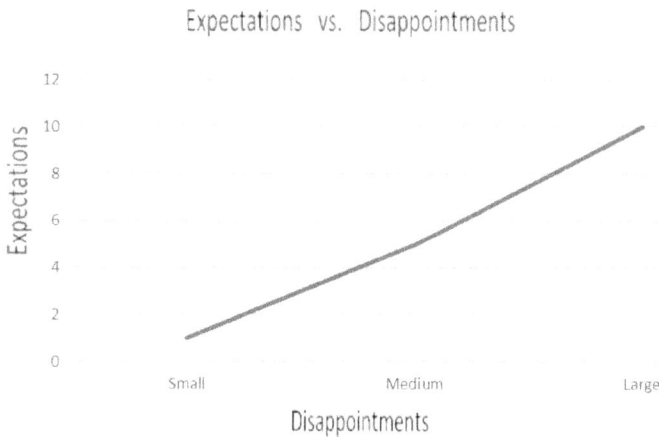

According to these two factors, we can see that Michelle received a large dose of disappointment; this was a shock to her trust meter, which eventually led to it malfunctioning. Now twenty years later she is in my office, her trust meter, as well as all of her relationships, is broken. Michelle's life has been poisoned from one broken promise made twenty years ago, a promise about a bicycle.

As I stated earlier, *What people don't do* can also have a long-lasting effect. If your trust meter, like Michelle's, is malfunctioning, I will show you how to repair it in the next few chapters.

CHAPTER EIGHT

※

Picking Peaches

"Forgiveness is the key that unlocks the door of resentment and the handcuffs of hatred. It is a power that breaks the chains of bitterness and the shackles of selfishness."
Corrie Ten Boon, Clippings From my Notebook

Have you ever picked fruit from a tree? Our backyard in Kempton Park was not very large, but we had about ten peach trees that fit within a small area. Every harvest season my dad and I would go and pick the peaches that were ripe. It was important to pick the fruit at the right time, as the fruit flies and insects would devour the fruit if we waited too long. Sometimes a tree would produce bad fruit, either the fruit was stunted, or just plain tasteless. Now at times, my dad would work with the tree, caring for it and giving it attention because fertilizer, water, and proper pruning could help the tree recover. However, there were times when my father would pull a tree up by its root after a few seasons of it producing bad fruit. Then he would plant a new tree. There was no use trying to fix the fruit when the root was bad.

Why is it so often that when someone is producing bad fruit, we try to change the fruit? We give people seven steps to control their anger, ten tips for overcoming apathy, or three tools to improving their sex life. Though many of these steps, tools, and tips help for a while, the amazing thing about fruit is that it comes back. Fruit is dependent on the root of the tree and the soil it's planted in (we will cover this in a later chapter).

The reason I started with fruit before showing you the tree and the root is that the fruit is visible; we can see it. The longer the tree has been around, the more vibrant the fruit. It is easy to take bad fruit off a tree so that it looks like the tree is healthy. The problem with this is that removing the fruit does not deal with why the fruit was bad in the first place. It is so much easier to pick fruit than pick up a spade and start digging at the root. Digging takes effort, energy, pain and time, and for many people, it is time they are not willing to spare.

Self-help gurus have become popular in our culture because they are the quick fix baron, the immediate relief, the "take a pill and see me in the morning" solution. We live in an immediate gratification society where we avoid anything that might cause pain, hardship, or require any measure of patience. 'I want it now!' is our battle cry, 'pleasure without pain' is our motto, and the self-help guru and television talk show host are our prophet.

When you picked up this book, many of you might have seen it as a quick fix to issues you've been holding on to for years. Others saw this as a way to immediate success in handling your emotions. But I need to let you know, if you have not already realized it, this book is not a seven-step plan or a quick do-it-yourself manual. I believe the principles within these pages will help you. I believe if you apply them they can and will set you free from your emotional baggage. And I believe that success and freedom are yours when you apply these principles, but there is no immediate solution. What I am talking about in this book takes time.

For some of you, the roots you will have to remove are large and deep like a large old oak tree whose roots have entrenched themselves deep within the earth. These roots are not easy to remove, it takes time, effort and even pain and discomfort. If you are willing to take the time, expend the effort and persevere through the pain and the discomfort, I believe that victory and success will surely be yours.

Dealing with the Root

I want to show you the fruit because you will recognize it. I want to show you later how to remove the fruit, but I am not a fruit picker, I am a root killer. I want to go after your roots; I want to help you get rid of them so that they will cease feeding the tree in your life that is producing the bad fruit that has slowly become visible. Many of us have tried to hide the fruit, but it does not take long before it rears its ugly head for others to see. We might be able to hide it from acquaintances or those we work with or go to school with, but as soon as people become close to us, it becomes extremely hard to hide our bad fruit.

Now let me make it clear in case you are asking the question, "Why are you talking about fruit, I'm not a tree, and I don't have fruit?" When I speak about fruit, I am talking about our behaviors, the way we behave with ourselves in the privacy of our own lives and the way we behave with others.

Behaviors that are produced by a bad root are destructive and can cause harm to us and others. This fruit produced by the roots we will be discussing in the next few chapters are called resentment. Resentment flourishes when we don't deal with our roots; it is visible for all those who dare to look. I have divided the fruit of resentment into three subcategories of fruit:

1. Display Behaviors
2. Covert Behaviors
3. Addictive Behaviors

Display Behaviors

These behaviors are like a peacock; they are on display for everybody to see. They are hard to hide. Usually, the people closest to us are the first to see them, but eventually, they spill out onto everybody. As a peacock that struts its stuff, display behaviors are hard to miss. A few examples of these behaviors are:

- Anger
- Violence towards others
- Sulking
- Crying (Not due to emotional or physical hurt, rather used as a tool for manipulation)
- Bullying
- Heavy sarcasm
- Defensiveness
- Competitiveness
- Tearing people down, i.e., harsh criticism and words

Covert Behaviors

These behaviors are more secretive yet just as devastating. They can go undetected for a length of time, depending on how proficient the person is in hiding them. Covert behaviors are a lot harder to expose, as they are in many cases a lot subtler. Some examples of these behaviors are:

- Unfaithfulness
- Lying
- Manipulation
- Depression (not medically diagnosed depression)
- Jealousy
- Distrust
- Disrespect
- Hopelessness
- Perfectionism
- Inferiority
- Poor self-image
- Poverty
- Fear of all types

Addictive Behaviors

Now I do know that all behavior can become addictive, but I have reserved this category for behaviors that are both extremely addictive and destructive. These behaviors many times start covertly then eventually become impossible to hide. They can lead to health issues and even premature death. Examples of these behaviors are:

- Alcoholism
- Drug addiction
- Nicotine addiction
- Bulimia
- Anorexia
- Self-destructive behavior like cutting

Even less evident in their immediate effect, addictions can also be:

- Hoarding
- Sex addiction
- Pornography
- Escapism including daydreaming, computer games, television, and work

As you looked at these categories, perhaps you saw some behaviors that you have been struggling with, so the next logical question is, "Okay, how do I get rid of them?" Remember what I told you earlier: There is no easy fix. However, if you are willing to work through some pain, exercise patience and put the time in, I believe— using a cliché here— there is a light at the end of the tunnel. In fact, this light is dazzling, warm, and full of peace and joy. It's a new lightness that most have not experienced, weightlessness few have enjoyed. A light that gives purpose to your life and one that encompasses freedom to be who you are made to be. The question is, "Are you willing to keep your eye on the prize?" Are you willing to make some hard choices, to pick up the shovel and start digging so that the root is exposed? If you are, then I know there is hope.

Let us identify some of the fruit that your tree is producing. You must have a clear picture, a 20/20 vision of where you are now, so don't feel bad about yourself. For a GPS to function properly, it needs two very important pieces of information: (1) the destination input (where you want to go), and (2) the current location (where you are at this very moment).

Without these two parameters, the GPS will not work. We know where we want to go, (freedom from the past, grabbing with both hands onto the future) but these first chapters have been all about where you have been. One of the first steps at an Alcoholics Anonymous meeting is for the attendee to introduce himself or herself and admit that they are an alcoholic. Without this step, the process grinds to an immediate halt. Recognizing one's weaknesses is not a weakness but a strength, a step in the right direction, a move towards the intended goal.

It is now time to be honest with yourself. No more pretense. Lay yourself bare, there is no one around, just you and the pages of this book. From the three types of fruit identified in this chapter, pick those that you feel you struggle with the most. Write them in the spaces provided at the end of this chapter.

The exercise is a difficult one and, if you are willing, you might need some help to complete it. We all have blind spots, so some of our behaviors might be invisible to us but believe me, others see them. It would not be wise to ask every person you have met, "Hey what are some negative behaviors you see in my life?" Ask people that you trust, people who have your best interest at heart. Yes, it can be painful to hear the truth, but remember you are not doing this to avoid pain but to face it head-on. Ask them, "Do you see anything in me that is a negative behavior?" Let them know that they can be honest and that you will not react or hold a grudge against them, that this is important for you to know. Encourage honesty from them and thank them when they are honest. You will already know most of what they tell you, but I do believe that there will be a few things that come up that have been hidden from your view.

This process of coming face to face with yourself can be a painful experience. Self-inspection can be painful. Remember that this process is not designed for you to fall into self-loathing or self-condemnation. Everyone has weaknesses; all of us were born into an imperfect world with imperfect people. We've all picked up baggage along the way, and we all handle that baggage differently. You are unique; this is not the time to compare yourself to others. Someone once said to me, "The reason the grass is greener on the other side is because of all the manure!" Other people's lives will always look better because we are good at hiding our messes from others. You know this because you've done it too, so turn away from any pity party you might feel like throwing, and turn your face towards your destination, it's just over the horizon!

Once you have recognized your fruit, remember roots determine fruit. Rotten fruit comes from a rotten root, while good fruit comes from good roots. As I mentioned at the beginning of this chapter, I am not a fruit picker, but a root killer and I am teaching you how to do the same. How do the seeds you received from the weapons we spoke of earlier turn into the destructive roots that rob you of your "Life Four" and put you at the bottom of the heap? We're going to answer that question in upcoming chapters. Now, go ahead and work on the fruit exercise.

Actions to Freedom

1. Display Behaviors

    _____
    _____
    _____
    _____
    _____
    _____

2. Covert Behaviors

    _____
    _____
    _____
    _____
    _____
    _____

3. Addictive Behaviors

    _____
    _____
    _____
    _____
    _____
    _____

CHAPTER NINE

The Soil of the Heart

"Your heart is a planter box for good or bad seed. Depending on the soil found within, determines which seeds will flourish."
Orrin Rudolph

"Identity please!" I was on a train between Germany and Austria on a backpacking trip around Europe. I was fresh out of University, and my friend and I had planned this trip for a long time. It was our coming of age, our time to explore and seek adventure, far away from parents, family, and anyone we knew. It was the middle of the night when the train came to a stop, and my cabin door was flung open, and two huge police officers stood in the doorway blocking all light from the train's corridor. I was a little groggy from sleep and surprised, to say the least with this intrusion into my cabin.

"Your Identity please!" The larger of the two German officers said, his rough accent making the request even more intimidating. "Passport and Visa for the Czech Republic!"

"Czech Republic?" I wasn't going there; I was heading to Austria. I had not planned to go to Czechoslovakia; in fact, I was not prepared to go to Czechoslovakia.

Before we left South Africa, we had meticulously planned our routes. Being a South African, almost every country we visited in Europe required us to have a Visa for entry, so we had arranged all the Visas for the countries we were planning to visit ahead of time. Czechoslovakia was not one of them.

"Ya, we are on de Czech Border, identity, and Visa please!"

There were two trains to Vienna, Austria; one was a little longer route around Czechoslovakia, and the other was quick and went straight through. I had accidentally boarded the wrong train, and now I had no Visa.

"You will have to get off the train!" The police officer barked.

"Is there another train I can get on to get to Austria?" I pleaded.

"I think one is coming at 6 a.m. tomorrow." He replied.

So, there I was, midnight at a closed, deserted train station, by myself on the platform, snow all around, minus four degrees Fahrenheit, waiting for a train that might or might not come.

"Who am I?" is a question often asked throughout one's life.

A story I read about Friedrich Schleiermacher, an 18th century German philosopher, illustrates this dilemma of personal identity. The story goes that Schleiermacher, now an old man, is sitting on a park bench where he was approached by a police officer who mistook him for a vagrant and asked, "Who are you?" Schleiermacher could only reply, "I wish I knew!"

When asked the same question, many of us would probably answer the same way: "I wish I knew."

Identity and knowing who you are can influence the depth of any emotional wounds you may sustain. The more stable you are in the knowledge of who you are the harder it is for one of those weapons we spoke about in an earlier chapter to create devastating wounds. We are more resistant, not impenetrable, but resistant. Identity serves as a bulletproof vest that we wear over our hearts. Yes, there are still bullets that can get through, but we have a fighting chance.

My wife and I were redoing our flower beds in front of our home. I asked one of the landscapers whether they would be putting a weed mat down to stop the weeds from growing. He told us that they preferred to chemically treat the soil as this was more effective than the fabric weed barriers. Even like flowers, weeds need a certain type of soil to flourish. Weeds are not as fussy as flowers, but the soil is still important to their survival. I've called this chapter "the soil of your heart" for a reason, our hearts are either receptive or resistant to the seeds the four weapons release. Knowing who you are is a chemical block to these weeds germinating. For the root to start growing it needs nutritious soil.

Unfortunately, we live in a world where identity theft is rife and not only in the aspect of social security numbers and bank accounts. Internal identity theft is more prevalent than physical identity theft in the lives of men and woman across the world who don't know who they are! When we do not know who we are, we are more susceptible to believing who others tell us we are. We see this all the time in the euphoria we experience when others pat us on the back and tell us what an amazing job we did or how amazing we are. We also see it in the deep emotional lows we experience when we are criticized or degraded in front of others or even in private.

We see it all over today's world as people are continuously trying to prove their worth to others by climbing the proverbial ladder of success. They believe others will validate their worth if they can get a bigger home, a larger television, a cool looking car; or they can get into the right social circles. I'm not saying that being degraded or criticized is right, nor that having a nice home or car is wrong. However, if these types of things give you your worth, then the soil of your heart is a breeding ground for the seeds released by the four types of weapons previously discussed. Our reaction to these seed releasing weapons (of what people say, do or don't say or do) are filtered down to their very core. The only plausible explanation is that we don't know who we are because if we did, we would be far more resistant to these weapons.

The soil that lacks the chemical weed barrier of good identity is the soil of insecurity. This soil is a breeding ground for us to get hurt because it has the perfect ingredients for the seeds that are planted in it to germinate and take root. This soil spurs people on to get caught up in the pursuit of empty practices to bring them fulfillment.

Mick Jagger's song, "I Can't Get No Satisfaction" echoes the human condition. Everything that he was involved with was leaving him empty. The search for satisfaction, fulfillment is ongoing within the human condition. We strive for it, and we produce new inventions to solve this dilemma. Our western society is built on finding peace and satisfaction. The American Dream, when reached and found to be empty, has produced an American nightmare of debt and medications to make this hamster wheel that we are on more manageable. Our not knowing who we are and who we are meant to be has set us on the road to find out who we are. Most times we are looking in all the wrong places. There is no satisfaction. In most cases, we find ourselves on a road filled with heartaches and disappointments.

Just as a gardener who prepares the soil through adding compost and other materials to feed it, when our identity has been stolen, it breeds insecurities that nourish the soil of our hearts to be more susceptible to the seeds that come our way.

What is insecurity? *Psychology Today* described insecurity as "a psychological disturbance that is now of epidemic proportions." In other words, more people in today's world are insecure than are secure. So, what happens when all these insecure people try to have relationships with all the other insecure people? More insecurity! As people are constantly trying to find their identity in others who were not made to be their source of identity, a breeding ground of insecurities is propagated and nourished.

People deal with insecurity in a myriad of ways. There are those who deal with their insecurities through stories about themselves that are not true. Those who use humor to deflect attention away from their insecurities. Still, others who focus on others faults by pointing them out. Some who verbally pull themselves down and even doubt their abilities. Finally, there is the final group who pretend to have no insecurities at all.

Of the types above, I dealt with my insecurities, and I had many of them, in three of the four ways. One of the ways I dealt with these insecurities was always telling other people stories of things I had accomplished that were not true. I embellished the truth and even made things up. For instance, during my college days I told all my friends that I was trained in the art of ninjutsu and proceeded to tell them all the amazing things I was able to do with my ninja skills. My best friend and I who was at college with me, still laugh about it to this day. In a sense this was not a laughing matter because this storytelling became a terrible habit in my life and caused a lot of damage and mistrust. I never knew who I was, so I needed to make a persona of someone I wished to be. I did not like me, so I lived in a fantasy world that made me feel better about myself.

25 Indications of Insecurity

1. They will constantly comment on the appearance or looks of other people.
2. They will tell you of all their achievements and will frequently embellish the details.
3. Amazingly they will find it hard to take compliments.
4. When situations become intense they tend to fall into name calling.
5. They will always find fault in your dreams and goals. They enjoy telling you why you cannot achieve them.
6. They are very bad losers. When losing they tend to throw tantrums or sulk.
7. They are even worse at winning. They love to remind others that they lost and that they are the victor.
8. If there has been a broken relationship with someone, they have no problem denigrating that person.
9. When they walk over others, they will always have an excuse for doing so. This excuse will always put them in a better light.
10. Even compliments are taken as having hidden motives or as sarcastic insults.
11. They tend to find comfort in the struggles of others.

12. They are good at bringing up the mistakes of the past and holding it against others. No mistake goes unnoticed from the insecure.

13. They will encourage you to give up on your dreams and goals, or let you know that you are a fool to believe what you believe.

14. Those that have very little are usually a target for ridicule or blame. "Look at those lazy people, if they just worked harder they would not be in the situation they're in."

15. Ironically, they will also criticize those with money.

16. They will feel jealous for and belittle others success.

17. They love to gossip. They will find joy in telling you hidden secrets about those you love or respect. They are not beyond making up stories in this regard as well.

18. Everything that happens around them takes on a negative vibe. The glass seems to be half empty most of the time.

19. They love to compare negative events to those they have broken relationships with.

20. They refuse to find anything positive in those people that intimidate them the most. Especially if those people are confident and satisfied in their own skin.

21. They're good at making idle threats when they disagree with you.

22. They tend always to have the last word.

23. They love to play the game of one-upmanship. "Anything you can do, I can do better."

24. They cannot take criticism or any type of negative feedback. This usually places them in an emotional turmoil and defensive posturing.

25.   When circumstances don't go their way, they tend to play the blame game.

This list by no means is comprehensive. Insecure people do not exhibit all of these. What I want is when you see yourself acting in one or more of these ways, you will take a moment and identify that insecurity is what is driving that behavior. Yes, we all have insecurities, it's part of the human experience. I have not met a single person who is totally devoid of insecurities.

Insecurity is birthed out of our assumption of what we believe that others are thinking, perceiving and judging about us. Insecurity is often our reaction to that assumption. We are reacting to something we have no control over. The sad truth is that most of the time our assumptions are wrong. Assumptions occur because of a damaged filter from past experiences. We now start to put thoughts and beliefs that we have about ourselves into another person's space. And because of our unhealed hurt and disappointments from the past, we begin to project our judgments that we have about ourselves onto others. Because we all have them to varying degrees, what are we going to do about our insecurities? We can use these insecurities to propel us forward, to better our circumstances, to reach our goals and dreams. Or, the other option is we can use these insecurities as a crutch. We can continue to lean on them so that we can avoid the truth and blame others for our failures and stay where we are. The problem with momentum is that there is no "staying where you are." You are either swimming upstream or allowing the flow to drag you back until you plunge over the waterfall of failure and disappointment. We must take personal responsibility. We can't keep blaming others. We are the ones holding on tightly to the rope of the past, and it's our responsibility (response-ability) to let go.

Since we all have this ingredient called insecurity that can salt our soil, the question is, "Can we do anything about it?" The answer is, learn to dig through the rubble and uncover our true identity. So, who are we, what is our identity? I am going to answer that question in a later chapter if you dare to read it. Remember once you know who you are you will never be the same again. This is dangerous because maybe you like who you are and maybe you don't want to change. However, for the sake of learning to make yourself more resistant to the weapons you will face in the future, and for you to change the composition of your soil, you must settle this question. If not, you will continue to repeat the same pattern.

Let us not repeat our past mistakes again and again. Let us start making the changes necessary now that can help change the results in the future. Too many people wait for the results to become devastating before they seek change. I encourage you not to wait for the kill shot. Don't wait for every good plant to die in your heart's garden before you start composing the soil with good nutrients. Put on the vest now so when those bullets come flying you have insulated yourself from their killing effects. Start composting now, so when the bad seeds come your garden will not be a hospitable environment for them to germinate.

CHAPTER TEN

The Rejection Infection

"When solving problems, dig at the roots instead of just hacking at the leaves." Anthony J. D'Angelo

One of my favorite take-home experiments from my days in elementary school (Primary School is what we called it back in South Africa) was the bean in wet cotton wool. I loved watching, as a normal bean would disappear into a wad of damp cotton wool and then suddenly (to my young mind's perception) sprout a plant. It was nature at its most mysterious. How did something that looked so lifeless, in a blink of an eye produce a living plant?

As taught, life is locked away within seeds, waiting to break forth into the world, eventually producing its little parcels of life to continue the process all over again. Once sprouted this life can bring much happiness and joy to those around. Apple trees, pear trees, sweet smelling roses and gorgeous alien like orchids are just a few examples. Conversely, other seeds such as poison ivy, stickers, weeds, and poison oak produce things that can cause misery.

For these seeds to produce life or death something must happen, in scientific terms, we call this germination. Like the cotton wad that acted as soil for the bean, the soil of insecurities— because of a missing or damaged identity—is the perfect environment for this seed to germinate. We do not see leaves or a stem once the seed germinates. The roots are the first things to appear within the cotton wool. These are the very lifelines for the plant to gather water and nutrients from its environment to draw sustenance from the soil around it. So, if the soil around it is insecurity, what then draws from these insecurities? What are the feeders to the fruit that will eventually be evident in your life?

Just as there are many types of roots within plants, there are varieties of roots that nourish themselves from the soil of our hearts. I will focus on two of these roots.

The Root of Rejection

The root of rejection, and just like a taproot, it is a single deep root that can be tremendously hard to extract from our lives. Taproots result when the primary root growing downward grows much larger than the secondary roots. If you have dug up dandelions in your backyard, you've seen their taproots. In gardens, carrots are even better taproot examples. The taproot can potentially penetrate the soil far deeper than the top of the plant extends into the air.

Almost everyone experiences some form of rejection at one time or another. One does not have to come from an abusive or dysfunctional background to have experienced rejection.

Webster's Dictionary defines rejection this way: "to refuse to accept, submit to, believe, or make use of, or even worse to spit out or vomit." Another good definition is "to be cast aside; to be thrown away as having no value."

This being cast aside can be a fact. Children who've been abandoned or spouses that have been brushed aside for another lover are examples of being cast aside. The feeling of being cast aside can also be a perception based on earlier experiences of rejection. For instance, someone who fails to be greeted by a colleague can perceive rejection taking place, even though the reality was that the person failed to see them or was caught up in their own concerns that it never crossed their minds.

I remember dealing with a young lady who felt rejected at the slightest lack of attention. She would walk into a room, and if people did not give her immediate attention, she would assume that all the people in the room did not like her or were mad at her. She felt rejected simply because she never received the attention that she craved. In turn, she would sink into fits of depression, tears, and anger. People felt like they were walking on glass around her, as they never knew when or what would set her off. Her insecurities stemmed from a deep-seated root of rejection caused by a deep wound planted many years earlier. Her parents had wanted a boy, and when she arrived, they were disappointed. They, unknowingly, planted this seed when she was an infant. Her parents loved her, but their disappointment had created a deep need for acceptance which translated into her grasping for the attention of others.

Guy Winch, Ph.D. in his book *Emotional First Aid*, tells of a very well researched psychology experiment conducted dozens of times. The "subject" (who thinks they are all waiting to be called for an entirely different experiment) is placed in a waiting room with two "strangers" who are actually researchers. One of them spots a ball on the table, picks it up, and tosses it to the other. That person then smiles, looks over, and tosses the ball to the subject. The subject then tosses the ball back to the first person, who quickly tosses it to the second. Then instead of tossing the ball back to the subject, the second person tosses it back to the first person, cutting the subject out of the game.

Dr. Winch then asks the questions, "How would you feel in that situation? Would your feelings be hurt? Would it affect your mood? What about your self-esteem? Would you feel rejected?"

As Dr. Winch says, "most of us would find this idea laughable." So what? Two strangers didn't pass me a dumb ball in a waiting room, what's the big deal? Who cares? Apparently, we do! What they found was something quite remarkable—that we as humans do care, far more than we realize.

Dozens of studies have demonstrated that people consistently report feeling significant emotional pain because of being excluded from the ball-tossing game.

What makes these findings remarkable is that compared to most of the rejections we experience in life, being excluded by two strangers tossing a ball is about as mild as rejection gets. If such a trivial experience can elicit sharp emotional pain (as well as drops in mood and even self-esteem), we can appreciate how painful truly meaningful rejections often are. That is why being dumped by someone we are dating, being fired from our job, having a parent through their actions reject us, or discovering that our spouse has been cheating, can have a devastating impact on our emotional and even physical well-being. Just as the definition says, many people feel spat out, vomited out of a relationship that their expectations told them should be safe and secure.

What separates rejection from almost every other negative emotion we experience in life is the incredibly painful impact it has on us and our emotions. Studies conducted by numerous psychologists who asked people to compare their personal and painful experience of rejection to their physical incidents of pain found that they rated the emotional pain of rejection equal in severity to the pain associated with natural childbirth and various cancer treatments.

Can this be? Can rejection hurt so bad? Most of us have never been shot or stabbed, but this is how most people describe the pain of rejection, akin to being punched, shot or stabbed in the stomach. It's interesting that the stomach is always used as the place of the pain. The stomach and bowels have always been associated with depth. We've heard people use the terms, "bowels of the earth" or "I felt that deep down in my stomach." It's interesting to me that taproots always go deep. This gives the plant or tree more stability and makes it less likely to be uprooted. The more you avoid dealing with your wounds, the more you find ways to ignore them, the deeper the taproot goes and the harder it is (not impossible, never impossible) to uproot it.

A person with a root of rejection always seems to feel as if something is amiss, like a piece of them has been removed that can never be replaced. They have a hole that they are unable to fill. There is an emotional deficiency, and essentially, they are operating from lack. It is their reality, their starting block that they launch from daily. Sadly because of this they are always searching and seeking for others approval and for acquaintances and strangers alike to determine their value. They put all their trust in those around them to evaluate their worth which ultimately leads to disaster. We should never let how other people treat or view us determine our worth. We must open ourselves to allowing growth in our lives so that we will become confident enough to believe that we do have worth and value. If others see us as less valuable, we are not the ones with a problem. Those who belittle and degrade others are only hiding their own insecurities and projecting them onto other people.

The root of rejection is nothing more than damage from a misplaced identity. Whenever we base our identity on somebody or something else, we make ourselves vulnerable to the damage of rejection.

Rejection is painful, so we develop ways to protect ourselves from this pain. Walls are built either to keep intruders outside or to keep prisoners inside. One of the big adjustments my wife and I had to make when moving to the United States was living life without walls. In South Africa, every home had walls. We were used to our walls because they were secure, high and offered some protection.

The first thing that I recognized as my wife and I drove into the suburbs of Longview, Texas was the lack of walls. "Where are the walls?" I had asked, "Why are there no walls?" In fact, there weren't even walls or fences that separated you from your neighbors. One yard ended, the other began. The only semblance of any walls was backyards, and even those were measly fences. In South Africa, our walls were thick, brick, high and imposing. My wife and I were used to a lifestyle of walls and security, and it was foreign and a little scary for us to live in a home where you could see the street from your front windows.

People use many types of walls to protect themselves when they have a root of rejection growing in them. Let us examine two of these protection methods.

Walls of Promise

Walls of promises are walls we build around ourselves from self-made promises. These promises or vows are commitments that we make to ourselves that sadly most times we break. They are promises like:

- No one will ever get close to me and hurt me again!
- I'm the master of my world; no one will control me!
- I won't be pushed around by anyone again!
- I don't need anyone; I can make it on my own!
- I won't believe another word or promise from anyone ever again!
- I will never be poor like my parents!

People make these promises frequently during their lifetime. The problem is that while we make them for self-protection, they can become vices that suffocate and potentially kill what we need most: good, loving, healthy relationships.

I watched a young man who had made one of these vows. When he was young, his parents never had much money. They weren't poor, but they had to budget for everything and many times he went without things that his friends took for granted. This perceived lack created resentment and wounds within him. The weapon of poison (*What people don't do*) sowed a seed into his soil. Eventually, he made a promise to himself; in fact, this promise was made many times aloud in arguments with his parents. "I will never be poor like you. One day I will have lots of money!" He locked into this vow and from that moment on his whole life became a pursuit of money, even to the detriment of his own family. In the Bible 1 Timothy 6:10 states, "The love of money is the root of all evil." In this young man's life that vow, which created a passion or love for the very thing he believed he lacked also created all sorts of "evil" in his life and the life of his family.

Another example of this is a young lady whom we will call Carol. Her friend's brother sexually abused Carol when she was a child. When she was thirteen her father had an affair. These events prompted her to make a vow. Her vow was simple, "I will never be hurt by any male or person in authority ever again!"

I watched as Carol started severing any relationship she had with any authority figure—male or female—in her life. She couldn't keep a job longer than six months. Her relationships with men were short-lived and usually ended in a great deal of pain and disappointment. Her relationship with God was cut off. Her relationship with her father was broken, and it just kept on getting worse. Eventually, she tried to commit suicide to end the last relationship she had, the relationship she had with herself.

These walls of promises we build around ourselves are powerful. They were designed to keep us safe, but all they do is create harm. What are the vows that you have made? Perhaps you need to think about some of the things you have promised yourself. I'm not saying that everything you promise yourself will become a wall. I want to focus on those things that involved a serious, determined promise, an agreement of sorts that you have made with yourself. These promises are decisions we have made concerning how we will take care of ourselves and protect our well-being.

Use the Wall of Promises exercise on the next page to examine the promises you've made to yourself. In the space provided write down the promise you have made to yourself. Once you have done that, write down the outcomes of that promise that you see in your life. I will start the exercise for you as an example.

Wall of Promises Exercise

My wall of promise:

- I will never be lied to by anyone in authority ever again!

The outcome:

- *A skepticism over everything people who are in authority ever say.*
- *A wait and see approach. "Prove it to me!"*
- *A lack of trust when it comes to leaders.*

Your wall of promises:

1. _____
2. _____
3. _____
4. _____
5. _____

Your outcomes:

1. _____
2. _____
3. _____
4. _____
5. _____

Walls of Self-Defense

Three major ways that we use these walls to defend ourselves is through flight, fight or become invisible. Either we go on the offensive, we turn and run, or we hunker down and hope no one sees us. Now, remember what we are talking about here are reactions created by and fed by the root of rejection. I am not talking about the healthy alternatives to fight and flight. Yes, I believe there are times in life that we need to stand our ground and times we need to back down. I believe in the cliché, "Choose your battles wisely." These, however, are choices made through and driven by careful thought and circumstances that demand action. When rejection feeds these self-defense walls, more harm is committed than good, and many times we are left confused and embarrassed.

Of course, the main way that we defend ourselves with these walls is firing from the ramparts. Anger is a commonly used tool. When my wife says things that are mistakenly taken through my filter of perception to mean that she is belittling me just like my dad did, I respond in anger. I defend myself. Anger became my main weapon of defense against the deep root of rejection I had inside me. It made me feel that I was in control because rejection always made me feel that I was never in control. When people I couldn't afford to get angry with because they could fire me etc. belittled me, I would hunker down and take it. Mind you, though, inside I would be seething because the anger was still there. I was good at internalizing it, keeping it locked away like a caged animal. The problem was that animal would always escape at the wrong time and usually it would be with those I loved.

I learned the hunker down behavior very well when I was young. When my dad would get into one of his tirades, I would stare at the floor, avoid eye contact and try to make myself as small as possible. If I was not attacking, I was avoiding, hiding, or laying low. I was afraid of confrontation, especially with those that were in positions of authority. My root of rejection wanted their approval; therefore, to confront them was not an option. In my mind, confronting a person whose approval I longed for was foolish. It was foolish towards my dad and therefore foolish towards anyone else in authority. The outcome was unresolved issues which would turn into the second root type: the root of bitterness, which we will discuss in the next chapter.

CHAPTER ELEVEN

Bitter is the Root

"The initial result of eating something bitter is to make you gag, but over time when allowing yourself to get accustomed to bitter tastes you can overcome that natural impulse. When we allow ourselves to become accustomed to bitterness in our life the resulting consequences are destructive and long lasting."

Orrin Rudolph

The second root is the root of bitterness. This root resembles roots called *fibrous roots*. According to Wikipedia's definition, "a fibrous root system is the opposite of a taproot system. It is usually formed by thin, moderately branching roots growing from the stem. The fibrous root systems look like a mat made out of roots when the tree has reached full maturity. Most trees begin life with a taproot, but after one to a few years change to a wide-spreading fibrous root system with mainly horizontal surface roots and only a few vertical, deep anchoring roots."

The roots of bitterness start to develop when you fail to deal with the root of rejection. Hidden or unresolved issues will always turn into bitterness, and bitterness is a deadly poison to you both emotionally and physically. One reason bitterness is so dangerous is because it can take root, grow and spread, and contaminate and defile your heart, body, and spirit before you even realize what's wrong with you.

Various Definitions of Bitterness
- Having a taste that is sharp, acrid, and unpleasant
- Causing a sharply unpleasant, painful, or stinging sensation
- Difficult or distasteful to accept, admit, or bear
- Proceeding from or exhibiting strong animosity
- Resulting from or expressive of severe grief, anguish, or disappointment
- Marked by resentment or cynicism

Bitterness is not something that occupies our minds. It doesn't announce itself nor fire off a warning shot to let us know that it has arrived. It sneaks up on us and like any parasite hitches a ride. Because of this, we need to educate ourselves about bitterness. What are the causes, symptoms, and results that it can cause in our lives?

When I was still at school in Africa, during our summer vacation which was during December and January, I enjoyed serving as a camp counselor at Mpongo Game Reserve which also served as our summer camp. The kids got to spend nights camping out under the stars among all the wild game and learning all sorts of survival techniques out in the African bush. Of course, we as counselors got to do all the fun things as well.

One year after returning home from the camp, I started to experience excruciating headaches and began to run a high fever. My body ached all over, and after two days without any relief, my parents took me to a doctor. After finding out where I had been for the last few weeks, he gave me a thorough body examination. It was during this embarrassing exam that he found a large African tick embedded in my scalp, hidden under my hair. He knew what to look for based on the various questions he asked, the recognition of the symptoms, and his knowledge of African borne diseases. When he found the tick, he knew that I had African tick bite fever, even before he drew my blood for analysis. Just like that tick, bitterness will attach itself to its host. It can remain hidden for years, but eventually, you will start to experience its effects, and they are deadly! So, let us start by examining a few things that we should know about this root of bitterness.

The Root of Bitterness

1. Bitterness attaches itself after its host has experienced unwanted failures, disappointments, and setbacks that are perceived to be beyond the hosts control.

    Like a tick, bitterness lies in wait for the right circumstance to take place. For me it was walking under a tree, my head brushing the branch on which the tick was perched. As we walk through life, there are ample opportunities for us to open ourselves to this parasite. Here are just a few examples when bitterness falls from the branches of life and begins to feed.

- When we feel that the experiences that have happened to us are the responsibility of others.
- When we no longer feel that we have control over a situation and the result is that we or others we love are put in harm's way or walk away hurt.
- When natural feelings of sadness or regret turn to anger, and this anger is not dealt with correctly.

2. Bitterness occurs when the host believes, rightly or wrongly, that others could have prevented the undesired outcome.

   Regret and bitterness are two sides of a coin. Regret is partly emotional as well as a thought process in which we believe that if we did something differently, there would be a better outcome. Alternatively, bitterness has a similar experience except instead of you being the one who was responsible for creating the outcome, someone else has created the undesired experience and hindered the favorable one. Bitterness feeds off a host who cannot get over the blame, and who sees themselves as a victim of circumstance.

3. Bitterness, much like other negative emotions, releases poison into the hosts system that can have dire consequences towards the health of the host.

   Just like that tick, while feeding on my blood, was releasing its toxins and disease into my system, so too does bitterness release a cocktail of emotional disease and poison into the embittered person's system. Research has revealed that negative emotions play a large part in influencing the release of stress hormones such as dopamine and epinephrine. Cortisol is another one of these stress hormones, and it is believed to affect the metabolic system.

Stress hormones act by mobilizing energy from storage to muscles, increasing heart rate, blood pressure, and breathing rate. They also shut down metabolic processes such as digestion, reproduction, and growth. Chronically high levels of cortisol, in turn, can disrupt other bodily systems, including one of the most important, the immune system. If this occurs, it can increase the host's vulnerability to disease. Medical doctors have held this opinion for many years. As I mentioned earlier, bitterness is a poison that not only affects you emotionally but physically as well.

> "Doctors have found that people who are bitter and have a lot of hatred in their hearts, have much more arthritis than those who are at peace. Similarly, they've discovered that those who have a lot of fear in their minds—worries, tension, phobias, etc.—have a lot more mental trouble and more stomach trouble, as well as more heart trouble."
> *David and Maria Brandt Berg*

4. Removing the tick was just the start, the host should take the antibiotic of trying to reconcile, taking some responsibility, and getting over the blame game.

Once again, personal responsibility comes to the forefront. I could have decided that it was the camp's fault that I got that tick. I mean, they should have sprayed that entire reserve with tick-killing poison. When we play the blame game, our attention is focused on the other person and not on ourselves and the bitterness growing inside of us. I could have decided that I did not need to take the medication my doctor prescribed. I could get better on my own. After all, it was their fault, let them take the medication.

I know that all sounds so foolish, but the sad thing is that's how people infected with the disease that bitterness causes react. Others can see the effects and the damage it is causing. However, embittered, those who are living with its poison are blind to everything except the blame they keep directing towards others. One thing I know is that in life there is only one person you can deal with or change; that person is you.

In 2003 Psychiatrist Michel Linden proposed a new medical disorder called PTED (*Post-Traumatic Embitterment Disorder*) defined as "a pathological reaction to drastic life events. The trigger is an extraordinary although common negative life event as for example divorce, dismissal, personal insult or vilification. The consequence is severe and long-lasting embitterment. This disorder is not "traumatic" because of the content of the triggering event but because of the temporal connection to the critical incident. Minutes before the person was healthy, minutes later he or she is chronically ill and severely affected." Patients feel embittered and downhearted, withdraw from social activities, complain about multiple psychosomatic symptoms, and harbor suicidal ideas as well as ideas of murder-suicide. They are often misdiagnosed as having anxiety disorder, personality disorder, or depression.

So how do you identify bitterness in your life? Here is a short checklist.

Bitterness Checklist

- ☐ It's poison; it eats away at you on the inside. A lack of peace and joy.
- ☐ Causes anguish and pain whenever you see, hear or speak about that person
- ☐ Is associated with jealousy and selfish ambition.
- ☐ Defiles others. You create a gang of bitter people, who surround you and all dislike or even hate the person you are embittered towards.
- ☐ Creates a withdrawal from social activities.
- ☐ Thoughts of revenge or payback towards the person who hurt.
- ☐ A choice or lack of desire to forgive.
- ☐ Creates over the top responses (Overreactions)
- ☐ People who resemble the person you are bitter towards, create in you an emotional reaction.

I would confidently say that if you checked at least two of the above symptoms, there is a good possibility that a root of bitterness is beginning to take root. If you have checked four or more, it is probably becoming well established in your soil.

Bitterness works within us in two major ways (1) what we feel and (2) what we think.

What We Feel

As this root starts to take hold and spread, we go through five levels of emotion.

- Level One: There is a pain in the pit of your stomach. These are the early stages and can be dealt with reasonably easily.

- Level Two: Starting to feel a sense of injustice. "This is not fair!" "This should not have happened to me!" "I don't deserve this!"

- Level Three: Frustration. "I have no control" "They've taken away my choices!" "I just want to scream!"

- Level Four: Anger. This anger can be outward towards others, or inward towards oneself.

- Level Five: Hatred. When we get to this level, all sorts of destructive and damaging behaviors start to happen.

Where are you on these levels? Circle the level that you believe you have reached. Remember, no matter how far you have gone, it's never too late to turn around, even if bitterness has landed you in life's worst consequences.

Not only does bitterness affect the way we feel but it also affects the way we think. Our very thoughts become negative. We are always looking for something negative to happen. Bitterness has tainted the lenses of our life. Life takes on a darker hue, and a negative taint clouds all we are involved in and all that we attempt. Please don't misunderstand me, not all negative people are bitter, but I do believe that all bitter people carry negativity. To them it makes sense if the "world" (through people) has done them in, then the world is an unjust place. And if this happened once, what is to stop it from happening again? Bitterness, as the definition implies, leaves a bitter taste in our mouths, a bitter outlook on life and a bitter oil slick on the surface of our existence.

Just as we peeled back the cotton wad and examined the roots hidden beneath, we find that both the root of rejection and the root of bitterness are but the start of devastation and despair.

The good news is that before the tree becomes fully formed and the fruit ripens, you can choose to take the ax to the root and destroy it before it has time to develop.

Even if the roots of rejection and bitterness have taken hold in your life, though the process is a little harder and will take more effort, it is never too late to start. For someone who has allowed these roots to flourish life might look like a miserable endeavor, but hold on there is light, a beautiful bright light at the end of this tunnel. Bear with me a little longer, because the consequences of letting all this stuff go, is a magnificent and beautiful future. You don't have to live in Einstein's circle of madness. You can let go of the whirlybird and jump off. You might be a little dizzy, but once you gain your footing, life will look very different.

Part Three:

The Road to Healing

❋

CHAPTER TWELVE

The Walk and the Talk

"There needs to come a time where you must let go. If you do not, if you hang onto unforgiveness toward yourself, others and the events that have transpired—unless you realize that the experience is over—you will never move forward."

Orrin Rudolph

Have you heard the story about a little boy and a caterpillar? I'd like to share it with you to illustrate an important point. The story goes . . .

"Once a little boy was playing outdoors and found a fascinating caterpillar. He carefully picked it up and took it home to show his mother. He asked his mother if he could keep it, and she said he could if he would take good care of it.

The little boy got a large jar from his mother and put plants to eat, and a stick to climb on, in the jar. Every day he watched the caterpillar and brought it new plants to eat.

One day the caterpillar climbed up the stick and started acting strangely. The boy worriedly called his mother who came and understood that the caterpillar was creating a cocoon. The mother explained to the boy how the caterpillar was going to go through a metamorphosis and become a butterfly.

The little boy was thrilled to hear about the changes his caterpillar would go through. He watched every day, waiting for the butterfly to emerge. One day it happened, a small hole appeared in the cocoon and the butterfly started to struggle to come out.

At first the boy was excited, but soon he became concerned. The butterfly was struggling so hard to get out! It looked like it couldn't break free! It looked desperate! It looked like it was making no progress!

The boy was so concerned he decided to help. He ran to get scissors, and then walked back (because he had learned not to run with scissors). He snipped the cocoon to make the hole bigger and the butterfly quickly emerged!

As the butterfly came out the boy was surprised. It had a swollen body and small, shriveled wings. He continued to watch the butterfly expecting that, at any moment, the wings would dry out, enlarge and expand to support the swollen body. He knew that in time the body would shrink and the butterfly's wings would expand.

But neither happened!

The butterfly spent the rest of its life crawling around with a swollen body and shriveled wings.

It never was able to fly . . .

As the boy tried to figure out what had gone wrong his mother took him to talk to a scientist from a local college. He learned that the butterfly was *supposed* to struggle. In fact, the butterfly's struggle to push its way through the tiny opening of the cocoon pushes the fluid out of its body and into its wings. Without the struggle, the butterfly would never, ever fly. The boy's good intentions hurt the butterfly."

As you have gone through this book, struggled through some of the exercises, and faced some of those packs on your back, you've come to realize that some of the stuff you have come face to face with has not been pretty. You have probably realized by now that you have gone through some hard times, some hard knocks, and a few painful experiences in life.

A Difficult Journey

So here we are. You are now in the chapter that I'm sure you've been waiting for since you started reading—the chapter that begins the journey towards that wonderful light of freedom. The last eleven chapters have all been about laying a foundation, a concourse on what has happened within you to bring you to the place you are.

For some as you read the first eleven chapters, maybe you never even realized that you were carrying any packs. For others, you might have known but didn't care until you saw the consequences of not letting go. For still others, you have felt the weight of those packs every day. You have grown weary while carrying them and you've been ready for this chapter since the beginning. Whatever your story we are here now. It's time to start the *walk and the talk* of forgiveness.

I must warn you: this is also the most dangerous part of the book. This is the place that 20th-century poet, Robert Frost, talked about in his poem, "The Road Not Taken."

> *"I shall be telling this with a sigh*
> *Somewhere ages and ages hence:*
> *Two roads diverged in a wood, and I—*
> *I took the one less traveled by,*
> *And that has made all the difference."*

You have two paths in front of you. There is a road that most people take. It's the easy road, the road that takes little struggle, and little effort. To walk this road would be the easy choice. Most people who identify that they do have unforgiveness in their lives, stop here. They turn back, they go around the track one more time, hoping that when they get back things will be different. It never is; it's worse. They try to avoid pain and run away from it which leads to a crippled life. Just like the butterfly, their wings never take shape. Life will always be viewed from a low point because they have lost the ability to fly.

We live in a world that preaches, "If it doesn't feel good, it's bad and must be avoided at all cost." A world that wants us to believe that everyone deserves a trophy and if it feels good, it is good. "Pain? Take a pill that will take care of it." Like the butterfly, we have countless people who cannot fly. Their wings are deformed because they avoided struggle and pain and took the easy road.

The truth is we need to learn to choose our pain. Pain is a part of life; we can't avoid it or push it aside. What we think is the easy way is the more painful way. You will have pain, and you can choose where you would like to receive the pain. For example, you can take the pain of exercise and good eating habits at the beginning, and believe me, for some people that is a pain! (I fall into that category). On the other hand, you can take the pain of a heart attack at forty-five, or all the other health issues that come with the lack of exercise and bad eating habits. You can take the pain of daily working on your marriage, dealing diligently with issues that crop up, learning to forgive daily or take the pain of separation, divorce, sharing your kids, and shipping them from one house to the next.

We've all heard the cliché "swimming upstream." It's never easy to go against the flow, to swim against the current. But just like the butterfly, once you decide to face these next chapters head-on, endure the struggle and the inevitable pain that you will have to confront, you will develop your ability to fly. Keep in mind that struggling is an important part of any growth experience. Once you soldier on through the *talk* and finally the *walk* of forgiveness you will be free.

In 1999, I came face to face with myself, as Michael Jackson so aptly put it in his song, "Man in the Mirror." If we can grasp the truth that the lyrics of this song preaches: that it starts with us, the person who is looking back at us from that mirror, then our actions and behaviors are the starting point for change. If we can learn to examine ourselves first before we examine others, change ourselves before we change others, then the world will be a much better place.

I still remember the day. A bright sunny day, I was driving home for lunch, when I received a phone call that would impact me deeply.

"Mom has been shot!" It was my dad's voice that came through the phone. The usually calm demeanor of my father was broken by panicked tones that were foreign to me. "You need to get to the hospital in King Williams Town immediately!" He then hung up. Thousands of questions were flooding my mind, "Was she okay? Where was she shot? Who shot her?" Fear gripped me as all sorts of scenarios were playing in my mind, but I had to push them aside and focus on getting to the hospital.

My wife and I lived in the city of East London, while my parents lived in a town 40 miles away. The drive would take me approximately forty minutes, which was more than enough time to be caught up in my feelings and emotions. I was hurt, I was fearful but most of all I was angry. My mom was a good person. She was always there to help someone in need. She was kind, loving and never said a hurtful word to anyone. Yet, someone had tried or succeeded in taking her life. For what? For what reason? I called my dad again.

"How is she? Who did this?" I blurted out.

"She's been shot three times." My father replied, "Don't know yet, I'm also on the way to the hospital."

"Who did this?" I repeated.

"She was ambushed at our farm gate." My parents owned a large poultry farm. "There were four of them. I believe they shot up the car, dragged her out and dumped her on the road before they drove off with all the farm wages and the car."

After I hung up, anger exploded in me, all I could see was my mom helpless in the clutches of four armed men, flung out of a car and left in a pool of blood on the side of the road. I could feel my stomach turn violently in me, my breath slowly being stolen from my lungs. The *garrote* was applying its pressure. Then something profound happened.

To truly grasp and understand this moment of clarity that suddenly descended on me from the heavens, I need to take you back a few years before this incident. It was January 1997. Another phone call, another tragedy. This time the call was from my sister. She was crying.

"Is mom and dad okay? Are you okay? I said a little panicked.

"It's Stephen!" She replied.

Stephen and I were not only cousins, but we were best of friends. He was closer to me than a brother. We had grown up together, went to the same school and just did life together. When one got into trouble so did the other. We had each other's back.

"What?" I asked, already fearing the worst.

"He's been shot. Orrin, he's dead!" More crying, then there was silence. I think, though, that my mind conjured up the deathly silence that seemed to envelop the room I was standing in and me!

Dead? Impossible! I just had lunch with him a few days before.

All I could think to ask was, "What happened?"

"He was ambushed coming out of a store where he was selling chickens. They were waiting for him!"

It was anger, blinding hot, seething anger, and it was the anger that I was feeling again two years later in a car on the way to a hospital, not knowing whether my mom was dead or alive. Was this going to be a repeat? Will somebody I love again be ripped from my life because selfish individuals who cared only about the money and their hatred of white people had decided to do so? In that lonely car two roads suddenly became evident to me.

Years earlier I had watched a man I respected, the father of my cousin, choose the one most traveled road. The one many of us have chosen whenever one of the four weapons mentioned in a previous chapter is used on us—the road of unforgiveness. I watched as anger, then bitterness turned to hatred and then how fruits of alcoholism, depression and some less visible fruit took hold. I watched him spiral into self-destruction, and no one could do anything about it. The further he walked down that road the more we saw it destroy him.

And here I was at the same place my uncle found himself two years earlier with two roads ahead of me: one well-trodden by the feet of the angry, hurt, and unforgiving people who had gone before. Now it was my time to choose. I stared at the mirror, and the man that I wanted to become stared back at me; however, there was another man there, a man twisted by hatred and bitterness, a man who was all about getting even, a man whose life had spiraled out of control. My cocoon moment had arrived, and I had to make a choice.

These moments, though maybe not as dramatic, happen every day. The more dramatic ones like the ones I recounted can have an almost immediate effect because of how impactful they are. However, the little moments all added up can be just as devastating or what the Chinese call Lingchi.

"Lingchi is translated variously as death by a thousand cuts which was the slow process, the lingering death, or slow slicing. It was a form of torture and execution used in China from roughly AD 900 until 1905 when it was banned." Wikipedia

I have watched this "death by a thousand cuts" take place on many others and myself whenever we have chosen the well-traveled road of unforgiveness.

As I sat in that car, not knowing whether my mother was alive or dead, I made a choice. I did not like the look of the man who chose the well-traveled road. I did not want to follow in my uncle's footsteps. I recalled something a good friend once said to me after my cousin was killed, "Forgiveness is not about the other person, it's all about you!"

You see forgiveness is all about the person in the mirror. Because that man or woman staring back at you is ultimately the one that will take the most damage from the choice of the road you plan to walk down. Jim Beaver in *Life's That Way: A Memoir* says it this way, "Forgiveness is not something you do for someone else; it's something you do for yourself. To forgive is not to condone, it is to refuse to continue feeling bad about an injury."

I love what one of my life heroes, Nelson Mandela said, "Resentment is like drinking poison and hoping that it will kill your enemies!"

Therefore, I threw the rat poison out of the window. I didn't know who these people were who shot my mother, I didn't know their motives, nor what drove them to this act of violence. What I did know was that I was about to start a journey. The cocoon that I had to break through was not going to be easy. It was, in fact, going to be a mighty struggle, but I was not going to make it easier in the beginning by holding this anger and hatred in my soul. For unforgiveness, will open the cocoon wide for you to slip out, but you have just severely handicapped yourself.

"I choose to forgive them!" I said into the air around me. "I forgive them for shooting my mom. I forgive them for potentially killing my mother. I release them and let them go!" Words, yes, they were just words, but when I spoke them something inside me broke, and I felt the anger and the bitterness seep out like the puss of a boil that's just been lanced. Grief and tears replaced my anger, but these were needed for my ultimate healing. What I didn't realize then was I had taken the first step in the act of forgiving, *the talk*. What I was about to discover was that that was the easy part. *The walk* of forgiveness is a lot harder, especially if you have walked some ways down the path that everyone travels. To turn around and walk back can be difficult, but that's part of breaking the cocoon and squeezing out that last bit of fluid into your wings so that you can fly again!

CHAPTER THIRTEEN

Of Debt and Invoices

*"The price you must pay for your own liberation through
another's sacrifice is that you in turn must be willing to liberate
in the same way, irrespective of the consequences to yourself."*
Dag Hammarskjöld, Markings

I once worked for a company that sent out automated invoices monthly. They used accounting software to generate and print the invoices overnight. Every morning when I came into work, there were a pile of invoices lying in the printer tray ready to be placed in envelopes and mailed to the recipients. I remember fielding phone calls from people who would tell me that the intended recipients were no longer at the residence or place of business. I even received a call informing me that the invoices intended recipient had passed on. The funny thing was that though some of these invoices were eventually corrected and sent to the right address, others just kept being sent, which resulted in many a disgruntled phone call. Since the invoices were automated, they were sent out if there was a debt to be paid.

Sound familiar? It probably should. When someone uses one of the weapons against you, after the initial shock of wounding, you begin to feel owed a debt. They owe you for the pain and disappointment. They owe you! You start sending out these invoices immediately, and they will keep going out until you decide to put a stop to it. This process of sending out these invoices is not only unproductive, but it is also draining, and frustrating.

Now the reality is that they can never repay you to your ultimate satisfaction. Even if they apologized, would you be satisfied with that? What do mere words mean when someone has created a deep wound, a painful laceration to your very heart and soul? Though words and actions can create great damage very quickly, words or actions from those who created the damage in the first place do not heal that damage as speedily.

Dr. Willard Harley and Stephen Covey, both talk about the concept of the "Love Bank" in their books: *His Needs, Her Needs* and *The 7 Habits of Highly Effective People*, respectively. I highly recommend both books. John Gottman in his book *The Seven Principles for Making Marriage Work*, tells us that for marriages to work well they need at least a 5:1 positive to negative ratio; this means you need five deposits for every one withdrawal. In this illustration, the mention of the 5:1 ratio, though in the context of marriage, means for every withdrawal that takes place, i.e., negative experiences like using our weapons, five deposits need to be reciprocated to bring the account back to where it was before the withdrawal. I believe that though this is a baseline idea the concept is sound in all walks of life. It seems that to right the wrong of a negative experience caused by words and actions, the new behavior must be so much more intense than the initial word or action that caused the wounding. This intensity is impossible to achieve, especially if the individual that was hurt does not choose to cancel the debt.

Sometimes these debts are held long after the person who owes the debt is gone. However, it does not matter whether they are dead or alive because there is a demand for retribution in you, and those invoices are continuously sent out demanding payment. You're in a vicious cycle as these invoices keep being returned and sent out again creating a boomerang effect of dissatisfaction that drains your energy. Besides, the more that these invoices are "returned to sender" the more the anger builds. It is time to break the insanity, as Albert Einstein told us to do.

So how do we cancel these debts? I hope that in the last twelve chapters you have come to a revelation of the why and the what! Therefore, with that in mind, we need to move on to the how. This process is broken up into two parts, the *Talk* and the *Walk* of forgiveness. The *Talk* consists of seven principles that will aid you in this process of freedom.

The Seven Principles of the *Talk* of Forgiveness

1. Get alone with yourself
2. Prepare to do business
3. Deal with perceptions
4. Create an invoice
5. Talk the talk
6. Destroy the invoice
7. Create a stone of remembrance

I have watched in counseling sessions as people of all ages applied these principles and experienced an amazing release of freedom flow through them. This *Talk* is not easy, however, as I have also watched many struggle through it. That is why I dealt with the chapter on choice. You cannot base this process on your feelings. You will never feel ready to forgive. In fact, there will always be a thousand reasons why you shouldn't. Your feelings will tell you a myriad of lies, so be prepared. Again, this process is about choice not feelings; this must be settled within you before you even begin. A mental exercise that I teach people to go through to prepare themselves before they take the plunge into the *Talk* consists of reminding themselves of five key facts, and I want to teach them to you.

1. This is not about feelings.
2. I have the freedom and power to make a choice.
3. Forgiveness is not about them it is all about me.
4. Forgiveness is not condoning their actions or words; rather it is not allowing their behaviors to hold me captive any longer. As C.R. Strahan says, "Forgiveness has nothing to do with absolving a criminal of his crime. It has everything to do with relieving oneself of the burden of being a victim—letting go of the pain and transforming oneself from victim to survivor."
5. My ultimate goal is to experience freedom from the past so that I can take hold of my future with both hands! (Begin with the end in mind)

Once you have prepared yourself, you are ready to begin the *Talk*.

Get Alone with Yourself

Though I have been in many sessions with people who were going through the "Talk," I've merely been a spectator to their freedom because this process is about them and coming face to face with themselves.

You have to allow yourself to look at the person in the mirror. You need to get alone with that person because it's that person who needs freedom. It's that person who is locked up and who needs to be set free. I always tell people within my seminars, "The person you are holding all this hate and anger towards is probably sleeping like a baby at night, while you are the one tossing and turning, plotting revenge or at least imagining what it would be like to get your revenge." Most of you won't have someone like me in the room with you, and that's okay. You need to find a place free of interruptions, a place of solitude where you can stare intently into the mirror!

This process is also the time to start bringing back emotions and feelings that for some of you, you have been avoiding or running away from for a while. Looking in the mirror is not pretty, but it is necessary. Some of these invoices have been going out for a long time, so long in fact, they are hidden deep within and conveniently forgotten.

In this place with no one around to judge you, it is time to dredge these memories up from the depth. I found that starting with the most recent memories help. Close your eyes, take a few deep breaths relax and start searching your emotions. Believe me, when I say this, as you start latching on to these events and emotions, it's like a chain reaction, one emotion, one event, leads to the next. As you start recalling events and emotions, you're going to write them down on your invoice that I will explain in principle four.

Prepare to Do Business

I hope that by now you are serious about your freedom, but if not, this is the time to remind yourself of the consequences of not doing anything. Remember what you learned from previous chapters: there are serious consequences for not taking action. Preparing to do business simply means to brush off all passivity, fatalism, and victimhood, and be prepared to face whatever may come with a determined set of the jaw, the grit of the teeth and a steely gaze (to mention a few clichés).

Dealing with Perceptions

Allowing yourself to come to an understanding that how you have perceived things may not be the pure truth is a major hurdle within this *Talk* of forgiveness. Just because you think it's the truth, just because you felt you judged the situation correctly, does not mean you did. In fact, as mentioned before our perceptions of situations are mostly incorrect because we never have all the facts. We are not mind readers nor are we omniscient; therefore, the chances of us misinterpreting a situation is highly likely. If we can agree to this, if we can come to an agreement that the probability of us misjudging someone's intentions or someone's motives are highly likely, we will be placed firmly on the path to being able to cancel the debt owed.

Create an Invoice

As mentioned in principle one, this is where we get to the meat of these principles: identifying the invoices that we have constantly sent out to our debtors. As the memories start to flood back, you need to write them down. Get a piece of paper and create headings as shown in the example provided. I have also given you two examples from my invoice to help illustrate what you need to do.

Divide your paper into four columns:

- Debt/Debtors: Under this heading write down the names of the people that have hurt you. Some of these people might be nameless. If that is the case, as you see from my example, describe the person or persons: their gender, race, age or even their smell. There are no limits to these descriptions. The descriptions are important if you don't know them by name because these descriptions can also identify why there might be some biases towards other people with the same description. I've seen people who do not know why they hate a person at work who hasn't done anything to them. Later they find out that that person reminds them of the one who hurt them deeply. There are all sorts of ramifications to this, which I will speak about in a later chapter.
- What they did: Which weapon did they use on you? The two examples I give were both 'Garrotes.' What actions or words, or lack of actions or words created the wounds in the first place? For some of you, this will be tough because recalling past hurt is not an easy task. But you need to

squeeze through the cocoon—it's for your own good. If you have been avoiding these memories for a long time, an avalanche of emotion can take place, so don't be surprised.

- Emotion: Write down the emotion you felt when the event took place, not the emotion you feel at the time of creating the invoice. However, many times these emotions mirror one another. I've seen people, as they write down these events, start to feel the same emotion that they felt at the time of the wounding. Remember the emotion is part of the fruit that has been produced by the roots that have grown deep within you over many years. Don't allow these emotions to alarm you; they are part of the natural process.

- Age/Year: Write down how old you were when these events occurred, or the year in which they occurred or both to put the timeline of events into perspective. It also helps you come to a clear realization of how long you have been holding some of these resentments.

Below is an excerpt out of an invoice that I created many years ago.

Debt/Debtor	What They Did	Emotion	Age/Year
Dad	Hit me in my face in front of my friends	Embar-rassment	18 years
African men	Shot my mother	Anger, hatred, revenge	1999

Talk the Talk

I watched a young woman go through this process. Her grandfather started sexually abusing her when she was four years old. The abuse did not end until she was sixteen, and then only because of his arrest. The first four steps had already been difficult for her, but when she began to write down the events on the invoice, her emotions started to bubble over. She wrote, "Grandfather" under Debtor. Under, 'What They Did' she wrote, "Sexually abused me." I could see the pain etched on her face as the memories came flooding back. Under 'Emotion' she wrote, "Betrayal, anger, help-lessness, fear, shame, and guilt." Under 'Age or Year,' she de-scribed it as "All my life." To this young girl, eighteen at the time, in her perception of life, these events had taken up all of her lifespan.

Writing the invoice was difficult, but the next step for her (and I'm going to assume for most of you as well) was the most difficult part of the *Talk* of forgiveness. Remember, unforgiveness is hold-ing on to a debt someone owes you. It is the constant sending out of invoices, like the one above, demanding payment. The problem as we have discovered is that this debt will never be repaid to your ultimate satisfaction. So, what do we do? We can either go through the process repeatedly, never finding the satisfaction or solution to that which we crave, even if we get revenge. As Confucius said, "When looking for revenge, dig two graves!" Alternatively, we can release and cancel the debt.

The *Talk* of forgiveness is a verbal releasing and canceling of a debt. It's the release of words that should have been spoken for a long time but because of either ignorance or stubbornness have not. I believe there is power in the tongue. Our words have the power to bind others or ourselves or set others or us free. Just as we discovered earlier the power in which words or lack of them can cause wounding, there is also a healing power in our words. This healing power is not only for others but us as well. This *Talk* has two parts.

Internal Expression

Internal express takes place in a private setting. No one has to be around for this part of the *Talk* because this is between you, yourself and you! Even though this takes place while you are alone, there can still be an immense struggle waged within the mind and the emotions. When the young woman I mentioned above got to this part of the exercise, I could see the struggle taking place visibly within her.

I told her to speak aloud, to say, "Grandfather, I forgive and release the debt that you owe me. I forgive you for sexually abusing me all of my life, and I cancel this debt!"
"I can't," she said
I reminded her of the five key facts and asked her to repeat the *Talk* of forgiveness after me.
Again, she responded, "I can't!"
"Remember, forgiveness is not about him, it's about your freedom."
"I don't want to!"
"Forgiveness is a choice, not a feeling."
"I'm afraid!"

"This is about your future and not allowing yourself to continue as a victim rather as a victor!"

She was silent for a few seconds, and then hesitantly she started to repeat the words. "Grandfather, I forgive and release the debt that you owe me." Tears were now freely flowing, as she started to tremble. "I forgive you for sexually abusing me all of my life." Now she started to sob, her whole body shaking violently. Through the sobs, she finally got out the last few words. "I cancel this debt!"

The emotion that I know that this young woman had held back for years finally poured out of her, a waterfall of emotion. Anger, guilt, shame and all the other feelings were etched on her face. Later she told me that it was like a dam wall that had broken. She said that when it was done, she felt spent, but in a positive, exhilarating way. A drowning victim had been rescued and brought to the surface, taking a huge gulp of life-giving air—all the poison that had been eating at her purged from her system.

For those of you who are skeptical that a mere sentence can have this effect, I have seen this scenario repeated multiple times, not only in others but also in my own experiences with this *Talk* of forgiveness. If there is no emotion released when you cancel the debt, it does not mean that this process has not been successful. The process is not about the emotion, even though emotions can be released, it is about a choice you are making to release yourself from the prison that unforgiveness has held you in so that you are free to fly!

The make-up of this sentence is simple. Speak out the person's name, and then repeat what they have done to wound you and when they did it. Once you have done that proclaim your forgiveness and the willingness to cancel the debt.

External Expression

This step is where I get the most resistance, and it is where many people draw the line. When they do, it's an indication that they have not taken the second principle to heart, "Prepare to do business." Talking the talk of forgiveness in the privacy of your secret place or as I've called it the 'Internal Expression' is necessary. The external expression of forgiveness is equally necessary. What is the external expression of forgiveness, and why is it so difficult for individuals to take this step? Because this is where you come face to face with the person or persons you've crossed the street to avoid this is the part of the *Talk* where you confront your debtor.

Confront, might be a little too aggressive a word, but that's what you are doing. You are not confronting the person or persons through accusation, but rather through recounting what happened, how it affected you and finally releasing forgiveness toward them. Yes, you heard me correctly, it is critically important for you to release this forgiveness to those that you have been resenting for so long. This step is where you need to keep those five facts about forgiveness squarely in front of you, for if you do not, you will not be able to complete this task.

You can conduct external expression in three ways. The first is face to face, verbally. The second, by phone, and the third by letter. I recommend the first and there are two factors that would dictate using the second method:

- o Distance – The individual or individuals are not close by and seeing them would require great expense in travel.
- o Safety – The individual or individuals have displayed violence, are in prison or in a mental institution, etc. and seeing them would cause safety concerns.

The factors that would dictate using the third method:

- o Safety – As mentioned above
- o Deceased, Location Unknown – You won't mail this letter, but instead write one as if you were going to send it, share what they did, what it caused and that you forgive them and cancel their debt.
- o They do not want to see or speak to you. They might not even read your letter but send it anyway. You are removing the ball from your court.

Your external expression is not about getting a positive response or, in fact, any response. Remember, this is all about you. It is about once again taking control of your destiny and refusing to remain a victim. Some debtors will respond positively, others negatively. It does not matter what their response is or isn't because this is not about them.

Destroy the Invoice

Destroying the invoice sounds simple, and it can be. However, simple or difficult you must do it. By this very act, you are making a statement that these events will no longer control your life. It is an act of resolve and finality, a statement of freedom. You are moving on. When I did this, I didn't just rip up the paper; I burnt it. I recommend you do the same. There is something about the destruction of fire which creates an indelible impression. Burn the invoice. Also, be sure to destroy your letter if you used the last method to forgive the debt of a deceased individual or a person whose location is unknown.

Create the Stone of Remembrance

Throughout the world, we see stones and statues erected to commemorate an individual or to bring to remembrance a deed or action of history, positive or negative. These memorials are there lest we forget the events or people of the past and their deeds. Why? Mainly so that we do not forget history, but to some extent, so that we can either learn from, repeat or avoid the achievements or mistakes of the past.

This final principle leads us firmly into the *Walk* of forgiveness. For as we walk in our forgiveness there will be times that we need to remind ourselves that we have forgiven. These stones of re-membrance that we create jog our memory, reminding us that we have forgiven though we have not forgotten.

These can be anything from a tree or shrub planted in your garden, to a bracelet or necklace that you wear. A few things though are uniform.

- It must be tangible
- It must be regularly visible

There is no use in having a remembrance stone that is obscure or hidden away that you hardly ever see. These 'stones' are there to remind you every time you lay your eyes on them that you have forgiven and that you need to keep on trudging the path less trav-eled, the path of debt canceling, the path of forgiveness.

CHAPTER FOURTEEN

❀

For Whom the Bell Tolls

"You cannot forgive just once, forgiveness is a daily practice."
Sonia Rumzi

Cornelia "Corrie" ten Boom was born in Haarlem, Netherlands, in 1892, and grew up in a devoutly religious family. During World War II, she and her family harbored hundreds of Jews to protect them from arrest by Nazi authorities. Betrayal by a fellow Dutch citizen led to the arrest of the entire family. Corrie, along with her sister and father, were sent to Ravensbruck, a Nazi concentration camp, for hiding Jews. Her sister and father died there, but Corrie was released, due to a "clerical error." Corrie later told her story in a book entitled *The Hiding Place.*

Corrie tells the story of a moment, years after her release from the concentration camps when she and her grandfather were together in Amsterdam.

"How do I know that I have forgiven the Nazi's?" She asked her grandfather.

"Do you hear the bells ringing, Corrie?" Her grandfather asked.

In the background, church bells were ringing announcing the time for worshipers to come to morning worship services.

"Yes, Grandfather." She replied.

"Tell me when the person who is ringing the bell stops tugging on the rope."

Surprised, Corrie listened intently to the sound of the bells that carried across the city. "There!" She said as the sound of the bells changed their tone.

"Now keep listening!" Her grandfather replied.

"What am I listening for, Grandfather?" Corrie asked.

"Listen until the tolling of the bells come to an end."

The bells continued to ring for about another minute until they faded away into silence.

"Corrie, you know you have forgiven" continued her grandfather, "When you stop pulling the rope!"

Pulling the rope—once you have completed the *Talk* of forgiveness, you don't realize that this is just the first step in this process of freedom. Once you have gone through the seven principles of the *Talk*, now comes the hard part. You must let go of the rope.

For most of us, the people that we have forgiven are not in another country, state or city. They are not unknown entities or even deceased. They are right there close to us. They are family members, work colleagues, bosses, friends or even neighbors, and we see them on a regular basis. For the ones we do not see regularly, that does not mean we don't need to let go. We do, but the saying goes, "Out of sight, out of mind" works, for the most part, to make the transition from *Talk* to *Walk* a lot easier. For those though whose debtors are right there, this transition might feel as if you have not forgiven at all, that you were kidding yourself and that what you just went through was an exercise in pure futility. That is not true, but feelings have been our guide for so long, we are used to them telling us what truth is and what it's not.

We must learn to keep our hands off that rope. Every time we see that person and the feelings of anger, or resentment start to spring up, instead of us looking at our remembrance stones and reminding ourselves that we have forgiven, we grab hold of those feelings. "Why not?" we might ask. "The feelings are comfortable."

Yes, it is true that these feelings have become comfortable to us. For some, we have nurtured these feelings for a long time. They are like old friends; in a twisted way, they are like comfort food. They have protected us behind their walls, and we feel safe in their embrace. Therefore, when they raise their ugly heads again, familiarity wins out.

I went through the *Talk* of forgiveness with an extended family member. He had acted in ways that had caused emotional harm to my parents. He was arrogant, prideful, selfish, and just downright rude in his behavior. All these actions and traits had, in my mind, justified my anger and bitterness towards him. These behaviors towards my parents had gone on for many years, and each time he would behave this way towards them, it deepened my anger. Many nights I would toss and turn thinking of ways that I could get even. The emotions that these thoughts would produce were exhilarating. It felt good when (if only) in my imagination I got even. Even after each phone call with my parents, when they would tell me of his latest exploits and behaviors and when my anger would boil over, I would get a high from the overwhelming emotion that I felt. I know now however that none of this behavior was healthy, but it felt good to hate him!

Though hopefully by now, since you have gotten this far in this book, you have come to the same conclusion that I did, that unforgiveness is harmful, and we need to deal with it. These emotions have been with you for some time. Many of you have carried these feelings for many years. They are like old friends. The problem is they are not good friends. They are those friends that stay in your house, abuse their welcome, eat from your fridge, sleep in your bed, break your things and then leave without a single thank you, or compensation for any of the damages they left behind. These friends don't just vanish after you have gone through the *Talk* of forgiveness. No, they are still hanging out, knocking on your door at all hours of the night, wanting in!

"Come on!" They say, "You know how much fun we've had together. It feels good; it's just right to have us back in your house. After all, we have known each other for a lifetime."

These friends' knocks become more urgent especially when you see that person or persons again, or whenever you hear their name, or see someone who reminds you of them. They even threaten to break down the door. Here is where choice becomes essential. You can choose to open the door to these bad friends and let them in to cause havoc once again, or you can bolt the door tightly and with authority tell them to go away.

"Come on; you can't seriously mean that I can control my feelings, do you?"

My answer to that is a resounding yes! Because if you let the same feelings in and as Corrie ten Boom said, grab hold of the rope and start pulling, the bell will never stop ringing. Each time when you get to confront the people whom you have forgiven, and you come out having kept your hands off the rope; you make the next encounter a little easier until the bell stops ringing all together and you can spread your wings and fly.

Unfortunately, that was not the case with this family member. I went through the *Talk*, but I found out in the next phone call from my parents that a situation had taken place that was hurtful to my mother. I was incensed, my friends were pounding on the door, but instead of telling them to go away, instead of taking a deep breath and glancing at my stone of remembrance, I flung the door wide and grabbed the rope with both hands tugging violently. The bell that had begun to lose momentum started ringing even more loudly and clearly than ever before.

The problem with pulling that rope again is that you negate what you have just done within the *Talk* of forgiveness. Yes, you heard me correctly; it's as if you never forgave in the first place. The wound that was on its way to being healed is ripped open and laid bare for the infection to start all over again. I know this sounds depressing, but I need to impress on you the seriousness of grabbing hold of that rope. When you do, you sink again into the embrace of those familiar emotions and they will drag you to the bottom again.

It took my wife to bring me back to my senses. I wrote a post on Facebook, to which a family member replied with sarcasm. My reply, for the entire world to see, was laced with bitterness, sarcasm, and anger. All my friends on *Facebook®* had the opportunity to see my dirty laundry. Everyone could see the poison. I was on the road at the time, and it was about an hour before I needed to present my seminar when my cell phone rang. It was my wife.

"I saw your post." She said.

"Did you see how I put him in his place?" I responded smugly. I never saw the poison, all I could feel were my friends having a full out party inside of me.

There was an uncomfortable silence on the other end of the line for a few seconds, "I think you need to delete that reply!" came my wife's response.

"What?" I was a little offended. "Did you not see what he said about my post?"

"I did."

"Well, I think my reply was justified!" I said.

"Do you think what you said paints a good picture for you and your reputation, especially since you are writing a book on forgiveness?" She said, "Does it come across as gracious, kind, forgiving?"

I was stunned. I never saw my response within that light. Everything shifted back into perspective; I realized my hands were back on the rope again and had been for a while. I had gone through the "Talk," but my "Walk" had ended abruptly. I had turned around charged back up the path to the crossroads, and then merrily skipped down the well-worn path with all my friends in tow laughing and having the best of parties. It was so subtle, so easy, in fact, to fall back into those old habits. The elephant had resurrected and was leading me where it wanted to go. Your elephant is always on the path of least resistance. My rider needed to take back control.

I went back to the *Talk*, with a determined mindset and my hands on the reigns and not on the rope; my familiar bad friends double bolted outside of the house. Then another phone call ensued, it was my parents telling me another story of this person's exploits. I had another chance to grab hold of the rope. I changed the subject. I was not going to get caught out again! I took a breath and chose the path less traveled.

In fact, just before this book was going into publication, this family member called me up to "let me know" what was going on with my parents. As I sat there listening to him, an internal struggle was taking place. My "friends" were using a ram to try and break down the door. I knew this was once again a test to "practice what I preach," so even as he was speaking, I was also talking in to myself mentally. My *Talk* was the talk of forgiveness, and that rope would not be grabbed again!

This "Walk" is full of those moments. Moments when choice hits you squarely between the eyes. You see them when you walk into the office. Choice. You see them when you attend a family reunion. Choice. You run into them at the store, movie theatre or church. Choice. What do you do? The rope looks tempting.

"One little pull won't do any harm." You say. So, you give a little tug. The momentum that was beginning to decrease starts all over again, and the next time it becomes easier to pull, and soon your friends have moved in again, rent-free, conveniently forgetting that you evicted them in the first place!

Now the opposite is also true. As you make these—sometimes daily choices—not to pull on that rope, that bell will slowly begin to toll softer until it ceases altogether. When that happens, you can run into that person, and those friends will no longer be banging on your door.

"So, what you're telling me is to forgive and forget?"

No, not at all. In fact, that little saying is another one of the few clichés that I do not agree with, along with, "sticks and stones" and "practice makes perfect." Forgive and forget is one of the dumbest clichés anyone ever created. The problem with this cliché is that the 'forget' part is not practical. The only times our minds forget something that has been traumatic or harmful is either when avoiding a bad memory or when there has been an injury sustained to the brain. For people to say "forgive and forget" is like telling someone to avoid the issue and hope it goes away or willingly take on a brain injury. "Here, have some amnesia for free!"

Now the latter is dumb, and the former never works. Have you ever tried to avoid a debt, hoping that it would disappear? What happens? You are eventually forced to confront it, and sadly, it has grown since the last time due to interest. The talk and walk of forgiveness is anything but avoidance and is definitely not about forgetting. As you make these choices, and the feelings fade, and healing takes place, you don't magically forget the event. What happens, however, is that through the process of the talk and walk you have removed the sting from that event. That wounding that you received from those weapons through the choices you are making is being allowed to heal, and soon even though that scar is prodded, the pain will no longer be the result. There still can be a slight sensitivity, but the sting has been removed. Humans tend to learn from experience, and sometimes painful experiences are good teachers. We will not forget, but we don't have to carry the poison within us through this journey of life.

There are times that I encounter those who have done grievous harm to me in the past. I have gone through the *Talk* and the

Walk" and come out on the other side victorious. When I see these people, though I have not forgotten what they did, those actions no longer carry the weight of the packs. In fact, for the most part, I do not think of those things when in their company. Now if that is the "forgetting" you are talking about, I can go with that. Those events are no longer at the forefront of my mind; they are bad experiences, painful experiences from my past that I have released, learned from, and they have benefited me within my character because I refused to become a victim and rather used the ability God gave me of choice!

My emotional muscles are stronger, my character is deeper and more developed and my vision for the future clearer and more pronounced when I've talked the talk and walked the walk. I have emerged on the other side better for it. My wings are strong, and I'm ready to grab hold of whatever the future might bring with both hands because my hands are free from grabbing the bell ropes of my past. I've thrown off those heavy packs and embraced the feeling of euphoria that freedom brings. I've evicted those who dared stay rent-free within my brain so that there is more than enough space to fill those spaces with those that I want to live there. How about you?

Part Four:

A Road Less Traveled-

For Christian Eyes

Only!

CHAPTER FIFTEEN

Rooted and Grounded

"So, that Christ may dwell in your hearts through faith. And I
pray that you, being rooted and established in love . . ."
Ephesians 3:10 (NIV)

So you looked! You might ask, "Why is there a section of the book 'For Christian Eyes Only?'" The reason is I did not want this book to be labeled "religious" or strictly for Christians only. Forgiveness is far too important a subject for people to miss out on because they did not want to pick up a book that has Christian connotations. As a Christian, I have found that I live in a perpetual state of forgiveness. My life is an example of one who, by the very nature of who I am, was desperate for forgiveness, and when I asked I received it freely and generously. I am no better than anyone else. I needed forgiveness and as His word says in Luke 7:47, "Therefore, I tell you, her many sins have been forgiven—for she loved much. But he who has been forgiven little loves little." (NIV)

When you have experienced much forgiveness, it is easier for you to love and forgive those who hurt you. I didn't say easy, I said easier. However, for those who themselves have not experienced much forgiveness, forgiving others does not come easy and can be a real struggle.

In Jesus' time, the Pharisees were relentless in their pursuit of the law. They showed very little mercy towards anyone that was different than them, that to them looked, smelled or sounded like a sinner. Unfortunately, in today's church world this can be said of many Christians as well. Their pursuit of justice and what they deem right and wrong according to the word of God brings very little mercy and compassion to those they deem as 'sinners.' As I stated before, when you do not feel true forgiveness, you feel that you must watch your step because God is watching you and frowning at the mistakes you make. You feel His displeasure at every corner; generally, you will treat others with the same stick that you feel is being used on you. The reason the Pharisees could not give mercy was that they had not received mercy. You cannot give what you have not received. If you are not experiencing the mercy of God towards you because of what Jesus did for you, you will not show the same mercy to those around you.

My father was not able to show mercy to me when I was younger. When we spoke years later, and as I listened to the stories of his upbringing and his relationship with his parents, understanding flooded in. My dad was simply repeating what he had received.

As my parenting life began, and my children entered the world, I promised (as so many others do) that I would not repeat the mistakes of my father and that I was going to be a dad who showed love and mercy in abundance to my children. However, there was a gap between what I knew in my head and what I believed in my heart. I found that on many occasions, more so than not, I could not show mercy to my children. I could show mercy to everyone else, but not to my children. I was beginning to repeat the same pattern. You can only give what you have received, and I had not received mercy because my father had not shown mercy to me. I will repeat this, "You will give what you have received." I saw my father pour out his anger on me when he disciplined me. He could never show mercy to me because he had not received mercy, so I couldn't show mercy to my children. I knew the amazing truth about God's grace, I knew the theology of grace, I taught grace and mercy to others, but I couldn't walk in it. My heart's desire as a dad is and will always be to show grace and love to my children. The truth is unless I allow God's love and grace to heal the areas in my life where I was wounded, I will always be trying to give out of emptiness rather than a fullness of love.

The Pattern of Fatherhood

Ephesians 3:14 – 19 is arguably one of the greatest prayers in scripture. So, it begs to ask why the apostle Paul started this amazing prayer, talking about fathers and families when he is about to ask for a deep work of the Holy Spirit within the church? In Ephesians 3:14 (NIV), Paul says, "For this reason I kneel before the Father," God intends for fatherhood in this earthly sphere to be a perfect reflection of His fatherhood. Paul continues, "from whom his whole family in heaven and on earth derives its name." If fatherhood takes its name from God the father, then I get my pattern of fatherhood from God as father. The reality is, however, that most of us get our fatherhood patterning from our earthly fathers. We have perpetuated the good points as well as the bad points from the fathering that we knew and experienced. However, we as humans need the work of the Holy Spirit to give us the revelation of the Fatherhood of God as father. We need the revelation of a God that is our Father, not just a God who has the power to bring correction to the imperfections of our fathering skills because of the way our earthly fathers related to us.

The main sentence of Paul's prayer starts at the beginning of verse sixteen and ends at the end of verse nineteen. God wants to do this by His grace; this is a gift. To be filled with all the fullness of God is a perfect gift.

Within these verses, Paul builds in a series of steps until he reaches the finale, "that you may be filled to the measure of all the fullness of God." Ephesians 3:19b. We will work backward to understand each of these steps that lead us to this incredible final statement.

Verse 19a – "To know this love (love of the anointed one) that surpasses knowledge," (It is only by revelation of the Holy Spirit, not by memorizing scripture or head knowledge) It doesn't come by understanding, it comes by revelation and revelation is given by the Holy Spirit.

Verse 18b – "to grasp (*comprehend*) how wide and long and high and deep is the love of Christ," The word comprehend means understanding to the English speaker. *Comprehend* in King James English is not the same as we see the interpretation today. To comprehend something in today's English is to understand something, as the Webster's dictionary states: To grasp the nature, significance, or meaning of (something). Breaking the word comprehend down into its parts we see that '*Compre*' means 'around' or to fully encircle, '*hend*' means to lay hold of, embrace or receive it. In other words, 'to fully embrace or encircle something.' The Greek word used in this passage is Kata (Kat-ah) *lambanó* (Lam-ban-o). Kata means fully, *Lambanó* means receive. To comprehend the love of God is not to understand it but rather to fully appropriate it, to fully embrace the revelation of His love for us. We are to appropriate it in our lives by allowing it to change us and to flow through us. In the western culture church, we have limited everything to our understanding of it. Knowledge and academia is the pinnacle of human development and achievement within our western culture.

Sadly, the church has embraced this type of knowledge as far superior to any other. We have raised knowledge up and placed it on a throne of its own, and if we don't understand it, we don't receive it. As 1 Corinthians 8:1–3 says, "We know that we all possess knowledge. Knowledge puffs up, but love builds up. The man who thinks he knows something does not yet know as he ought to know. But the man who loves God is known by God."

Knowledge has this amazing ability to produce pride, and in pride, there is no love. In fact, pride robs us of showing mercy and grace to others. God wants us to go beyond the limits of our understanding. The only time we will know the fullness of God is when we know the love of Christ in a way that passes knowledge! The only time we will know the love of Christ is when we recognize that we need one another.

Verse 18a - " . . . may have power together with all the saints." What the enemy has achieved, as mentioned in an earlier chapter, is that he has made a beeline for the roots. He has seen to it that we have been so wounded there, that we can't receive from one another in the body of Christ, and we miss out what God wants to put into our lives through others. As Proverbs

27:17 tells us, "As iron sharpens iron, so one person sharpens another."

So, here we are longing for His fullness, but He can't give us that fullness because we are not relating to one another correctly. There is a dimension of God's love that He wants to give to us and reveal to us. However, it can only come through other people we have a hard time dealing with because they remind us of some childhood hurt that we have received because of imperfect fathering. We wonder why we can't love others. We wonder why we can't receive from others. We don't know why we have a hard time relating to certain people. It's because there is a profound area that the Spirit of God is longing to invade in our life that all roots back to fathering.

It goes back to our growing up in our parental home and the things that were built into us there. Those things that have not yet been healed and transformed by the power of the Holy Spirit coming into our life. The Holy Spirit has not invaded our lives and transformed those childhood memories and things that we learned from childhood. Those memories and lessons formed us into who we are, but in Jesus Christ, we are a new creation (2 Corinthians 5:17). We're a child of God; we don't have to live with the imprint of our earthly fathers on us anymore. We don't have to succumb to the habits that were impressed upon us from years of earthly parenting. We can now live with the imprint of our heavenly Father because we were redeemed to be made like Jesus. We are transformed into the image of God's sons and daughters, not our earthly daddy's sons and daughters.

This amazing transformation can only happen according to Paul, "together with all the saints," and that is where there enters a big problem with Christians. I remember when I was a kid, we would play rugby, soccer or cricket with my friends at the local park. Cricket is a sport in South Africa using a bat and ball. We would always choose teams. The first kids picked was always the kids with the most talent at the chosen sport we were going to play. Then came the kids that were popular and finally those kids that no one wanted on their team. As Christians, sometimes we seem to transport ourselves back to those childhood experiences, picking and choosing who we would rather do church with, or allow into our groups, or even to hang out with. We pray even though we don't realize we are doing it, "Lord can I please choose the people through whom you use to change me and sharpen me?" The funny thing about the word *all* is that it doesn't leave much room for interpretation. The word *all* truly means *all*. So, if I could put words in God's mouth, I know from this scripture His reply would be, "No, if you are going to know all my fullness, it's together with all the saints, there is no picking and choosing!" When God does His healing work in you, you can receive from others again.

Isms

I was raised in apartheid South Africa. You can't help when raised in an environment of racism like that not to pick up racism. As a white South African, racism was part of the whole fabric of our culture. I grew up with the inherent feeling that as a white person I was superior to every other race and color. I grew up in a culture that never questioned my white superiority. It was a given and therefore if no one else questioned it, neither did I. Because of this superiority complex when I started to run into black Christians and other races that I viewed as inferior. I found it extremely hard to receive anything from them. What my father built into me and what I received from my culture and my forefathers were so much a part of my makeup that when it came to receiving from other races I could not. When a black man preached, I listened but could not hear. So, I kept to my segregated little group and lost a fullness that I could have experienced from others.

I can extend this to denominationalism, sexism, ageism, or even political party bias. It's not difficult today in the church of Jesus Christ to find so many "isms" that fight against us experiencing what Paul was talking about—fullness of God. We battle to receive from those from a different denomination, and sadly enough even from those who come from a church down the road, even if it's the same denomination. In the body of Christ, we could almost label it tribalism. Some pastors are so scared that the church down the road will steal their sheep. (They were never their sheep in the first place.)

I grew up with the prejudice that males are superior to females or are inherently inferior in their submissive role in the family relationship and within the church. I grew up in a male-dominated church culture that said a woman was inferior by inference though we never said it outright. By our attitude, we were saying a woman doesn't have what it takes to be a leader in the body of Christ.

I never saw a woman hold any significant leadership role within the church; the only people they could teach were the kids. Hush them up, tell them to sit down and shut up and make no sound. I was not only a racist to people of color but a sexist when it came to church leadership. It was all part of my culture. So, when I first met a woman preacher, I couldn't receive, in fact, I wanted to run out of the building.

You can't receive in the area where you have been wrongly parented, whether it came from your physical fathers or from the culture in which you grew up. Wrong parenting is that which puts into you the kind of prejudices that block you from receiving from "all the saints."

A Judgment Against God

John Sheasby, a powerful minister of the message of Grace and a father figure to me in the grace message also grew up in South Africa. Before moving to the United States, he shared a powerful story of how God had spoken to him and told him, "Forgive Me for making black people." When John heard this, he was rightly shocked. He explained that God had shown him that his (John's) judgment against people of color was a judgment against God. What he and I were saying when we were holding racism in our heart towards others was that God had made an inferior class of people because that was what our culture had taught us. And what God was saying to John was, "Your offense is against me because I made them; I created them. Will you forgive me for making a race of people that you have judged me in making inferior to you?" John repented when the revelation of this hit his heart because he started to see his stupid racism was nothing else but a judgment against God. John said, "I'm judging His creation." So, he prayed, "God, I release you, and I forgive you for making a race of people I judged because of my culture to be inferior to me." God replied, "I want you to forgive the blacks as a race of people for being black. You've made that judgment. You've judged them because of the color of their skin, now release them!"

And so, John said, "I did." God replied, "I want you to forgive every individual black person who has ever wronged you or hurt you." John concluded with "God then brought them all to memory and I forgave them."

When I first heard this story, something in me was exposed. I realized that like John, I too was holding all these judgments against people, not only based on their color but their sex, their denomination, etc. I could not experience God's fullness if I were not allowing God to use Christians of all races, colors, sexes, and denominations to minister to me and pour into my life. My "isms" were a major hinderance to my ability to gain the full comprehension of God's love.

The good news is that God is so merciful that He will pursue us and expose our cracked foundations no matter how long it takes for Him to do it. No matter how much denial you and I might walk in, God is too merciful to allow us to go the rest of our lives living in denial. He is too merciful to allow us to keep repeating the mantra, "I don't have a problem!" when He knows there is a cracked foundation in our lives preventing us from experiencing His fullness.

Rooted in the Past

Verse 17b – "And I pray that you, being rooted and established (grounded) in love . . ." so many Christians think, "I've got saved. Therefore, God has dealt with my past; I can forget about everything in my past and press on." The only problem with that thinking is that true spiritual transformation only comes through the renewing of our minds as spoken about in Romans 12:2. And the renewing of our mind deals with all the recorded memories from our childhoods. God in His mercy and goodness wants for His word (and the truth it contains) to impact and transform our minds and bring healing and real transformation within us. He wants the roots of our lives healed so that we can begin to bear the right fruit in our lives.

Many Christians have come to Christ and then found out roots are growing in their lives that they don't like. These roots are producing fruit that they thought had been dealt with. Then some well-intentioned Christian friend or leader—or even the person themselves ask, "Why are these fruits there?" Though we spoke about fruit in chapter eight, I would like to mention it again because of the way Christians deal with this fruit. The first thing we do is come to the altar and confess our sin and proclaim what a miserable failure we are as Christians and ask God to clean us up. Because of God's grace, we always get the cleansing we desire. We leave the altar feeling relief. We had our feet washed to feel clean, and then a few weeks later we do the same thing again.

Then a new teaching about strongholds comes into the church. Suddenly everyone has a stronghold so we come for deliverance. We get rid of the stronghold, and it feels amazing, but three weeks later we do the same thing again.

Isaiah 61:1–3, tells us about something called anointing where he says, "The Spirit of the Sovereign Lord is on me, because the Lord has anointed me to preach good news to the poor. He has sent me to bind up the broken hearted, to proclaim freedom for the captives and release from darkness for the prisoners." The progression here is important. For someone to experience freedom and deliverance, the first thing that needs to happen is that their heart needs mending. We can't proclaim deliverance to captives with broken hearts. The enemy will just come back in and reclaim ground through their damaged emotions. The anointing must heal the broken heart, so the captives can walk in freedom.

When buying a home, one of the first inspections the potential homeowner does is a foundation inspection. If the foundation is strong, so is the home. If a crack appears in the wall of your house, and you fix it, but it keeps appearing, do you keep fixing the crack, or do you start looking at the foundations to see what's causing the crack? A crack that keeps on showing up is a good clue that you have foundation issues. When bad fruit starts showing up, this is a clue that there are root issues. Do you fix the foundation and deal with the root or do you keep fixing the crack?

Where is Your Root?

This chapter is entitled *Rooted and Grounded*. Where are your roots? What are you grounded in as a Christian? You bear the fruit of whatever you are rooted in because the fruit comes from the root. In John 8:32, Jesus tells us that, "Then you will know the truth, and the truth will set you free." Now the truth can't set you free unless you expose the light of truth to the area that needs the truth. We need to get honest with God about those areas and become transparent before Him. Yes, He knows everything about us, but He is waiting for us to trust Him enough with those hidden areas, to believe Him, to believe that the truth of His word can set us free. If you keep shoveling dirt around the foundation and keep saying, "I'm okay I'll just keep dealing with this crack," you are showing fear and fear is the opposite of faith. We are afraid to look beneath the surface and expose that which is hidden there to the light of truth. When you pick the fruit from the tree, you don't change the root. The church has been good at picking the fruit but not healing the root of the tree. We are good at pointing out the sin, but not dealing with the broken heart.

It's impossible for the church to bear the fruit of love while rooted in rejection. It's impossible for the church to bear the fruit of faith while rooted in suspicion, skepticism, cynicism, doubt, disappointment, and unbelief. It's impossible for the church to bear the fruit of confidence in our heavenly Father if our earthly daddy bailed out of the marriage and out of our life when we were two years of age and deserted and abandoned us. Until you allow the anointing of the Holy Spirit to heal that root, you will continue to bear the fruit of what you are rooted and grounded in.

Vs 17a – "so that Christ may dwell in your hearts through faith." After reading this part of the verse, it begs the question who exactly is Paul writing to? Are the recipients of this letter Christians? And if so, why then is Paul writing to a group of Christians and making a statement like, "so that Christ (the anointed one) may dwell in your hearts by faith"?

The answer to that question is simple enough. The word heart here in the Greek is '*Kardiais*,' pronounced *kar-dee'-ahis*. The Greek meaning is a little more profound than the English definition. It means a person's center, their mind, character, inner self, will, intentions, emotions. In other words, when the Ephesian Christians read this, they would have understood that when Paul was speaking about hearts that he was talking about their inner person, which to them was made up of their mind, emotions, and will. So, when Paul wrote that "Christ may dwell in our hearts by faith" he was saying though you have received Jesus Christ into your hearts, you need to allow him into areas that you have never opened for his indwelling presence and for His transforming anointing power to change.

One of the areas that I battled was within my marriage. Whenever my wife brought up things I had not done around the house or said something that was in my mind not complimentary about some task I had done, red-hot anger would rise inside of me. Most times I would respond with a sharp retort or an angry outburst. My wife and I have got into some ugly shouting matches because of this. The Holy Spirit grabbed ahold of me about this, so I asked the Lord what was going on? Why was this such an issue for me? What was the root of this behavior? What I've discovered is that if there is some behavior that is unlike Jesus, get honest before the Lord and ask Him to show you the root, the thing that is causing the crack and He will show you. Jesus has come to indwell your hearts so that you will be rooted and grounded in love. He doesn't want you to live rooted and grounded in rejection, or bitterness. He has come to transform you, but you have to allow Him into those hidden areas, those areas that can be embarrassing or painful. We need to open up to Him.

Lord, Show Me the Root

So, I asked the Lord to show me the root. I did a check, and the check was this, "Is there anyone to whom I don't feel compassion flowing from my innermost being?" Compassion is the sign of wholeness. If you can have compassion flowing towards another person, that means you are whole in that area. When you think of that person and have no compassion for them, that is an excellent sign that something is wrong.

At that point in my life as I went down the list of people that were very close to me in my childhood. I knew it wasn't my sister, nor my mother; no, compassion flows freely for my mom. But when I thought of my dad, I knew the answer. In fact, every time my wife would make her comment, inside of me, I would want to say, "Stop trying to be my dad!" That thought should have given me a clue. God was showing me that I had never forgiven my father for never accepting anything I did as good enough and the way it wounded me and hurt me. So, I was responding to my wife based on what my dad had done to me. And the Lord just wanted to indwell that part of me that I would not allow him access.

Now, whatever it is, whether its memories, etc., that part of your heart that has not been opened to the indwelling presence of the anointed one Jesus is going to cause you problems. You won't be rooted and grounded in love. In fact, there will be a tremendous lack of compassion and love in that area. You won't be able to "comprehend with all the saints what is the breadth and length and height and depth and to know the love of Christ which passes knowledge so that you might be filled with all the fullness of God!"

Verse 16b – "He may strengthen you with power through His Spirit in your inner being." This a powerful operation of the Holy Spirit in your innermost being, healing and transforming you by the indwelling presence of the anointed one!

The spirit took me back to the moment of the worst spanking I had ever received from my dad. My mother had bought me a brand-new tracksuit to show me that she loved me. This gifting was not a usual occurrence as at that time my parents were not wealthy by any stretch of the imagination. To do this, some sacrifices on my mom's part needed to be made. As a kid of about ten years old, I was not very responsible. I was invited to a sleepover at a friend's home, and even though this tracksuit was special, and my mom had expressly asked me only to wear it on special occasions, I took it with me. I wore it the next day while my friend and I decided to build a go-cart, and the inevitable happened, I got oil all over my new tracksuit. I knew I was in serious trouble, so I made it worse by trying to hide it at the bottom of the washing basket. My mom found the soiled evidence and promptly burst into tears. When my father got home, he took me into the bedroom and took off his belt and gave my bottom a severe lashing.

My dad fathered me the way he was fathered. You know what I did to my daughter? In our first home in America, we only had two bedrooms, and my computer was in the baby's room. I would stay up late at night playing on the computer. My daughter, who was only one at that time, would wake up and cry. My anger rose in me, and I would grab her and spank her and tell her to "Shut up" until the fear of another spanking shut her up, or my wife came wanting to know what I had been doing. I would say that my daughter was being difficult. But she had been spanked and was now crying, and that was child abuse. You see, I was fathering her the way I was fathered, and I had never allowed Jesus, the anointed one, to indwell that area.

Praise the Lord that is over and that my girls are healed, my father is healed and so am I. Jesus healed and strengthened my inner being. He strengthened me to overcome my weakness of succumbing to my anger. He strengthened me to overcome my weakness of allowing the things of the past to continue in the present. We can put a stop to this whole lousy pattern. We don't have to live rooted and grounded in anger and hostility and rejection and all the other garbage because Jesus has come and by a mighty work of the Spirit, we can have the roots changed. Jesus, the anointed one, can remove the soil of rejection and bathe our roots in His deep abiding love.

What the Holy Spirit showed me was all that stuff I suppressed was still inside me. The only way the anger, bitterness, and rejection could come out was through the grace of God's forgiveness and my willingness to forgive those who have wronged me. All that anger was really against my father, and it was exploding out against my children. I was making my children pay the debt that my father owed me. The anger that I vented on my children was unresolved anger towards my father. Now that I was in the position of power, I began venting it on my children. All this was just the bent up unresolved emotions that were never submitted to the power of the anointed one and His love because I'd never walked in forgiveness towards my father and never allowed my heavenly Father to heal my broken heart.

Verse 16a – "I pray that out of His glorious riches, that he may grant you." All of this is a gift. It's according to the riches of His glory, not ours. How rich is God in glory? Paul wanted to show us that there is no limitation. God has no limitations on what He can give us. His glory is limitless. If our healing were dependent on the riches of our glory, we would be in serious trouble. He wants to do the work through the riches of His glory. There is no limitation; there is not one of us who has done or has gone through anything that His grace cannot heal. The indwelling presence of Christ, the fullness of God, is not just for Christians to say, "I've got Jesus living in my heart." It's for opening up every area of our hearts to Christ and His love to heal the roots and foundations of who we are.

God is making for Himself a glorious temple. He is making a temple that is not built with human hands as stated in Acts 17:24 but temples made of flesh (1 Corinthians 6:19) so fitted together (Ephesians 2:21–22) that is so connected to Jesus, the cornerstone and the anointed one, and fitted together according to the word of God (Ephesians 4:16) by love. Love is the glue that cements us all together, but what has happened is that we are so full of our hurts and wounds that we cannot receive from one another and therefore miss the fullness that God wants to give us.

CHAPTER SIXTEEN

Binding and Loosing

"I tell you the truth, whatever you bind on earth will be bound in heaven, and whatever you loose on earth will be loosed in heaven." Matthew 18:18 (NIV)

My family and I live on a small lake out in the country. One of the residents of this lake was an ornery goose that we nicknamed Grampa. One day we noticed that Grampa was limping badly and was bleeding. On closer inspection, we noticed that he had some wire wrapped around one of his legs. The wire was cutting into his leg and creating pain and limited motion. After chasing and cornering Grampa, and after a lot of honking and biting we were finally able to release him from his bindings and to the best of our mediocre veterinary skills clean and disinfect the wound before we let him go. Grampa limped around for the next week or two, but eventually, his wound healed and he regained his full range of motion. I must say, his ornery attitude never disappeared towards us even though we had helped him.

There is a power to learning to let people go, to release them from their debts toward you and to bring healing and restoration that brings change. This release is not dependent on the attitude of the person we are releasing. They might be like old Grampa, ornery and ungrateful, but we don't need to keep perpetuating the patterns in which we were raised and keep marring and scaring generation to generation. We can stop the cycle through forgivingness and the delivering power of the Spirit and the healing power of the anointing. I want to encourage you to believe for a new and fresh beginning in your family.

Matthew 18:15 Jesus, who is in the midst of a chapter dealing with offenses says, "If your brother sins against you, go and show him his fault, just between the two of you. If he listens to you, you have won your brother over." One crucial point to make here is that when you go and tell the person who has hurt you their fault, you are not going to accuse them. The disciples understood what Jesus was saying because in verse 21 of Matthew 18, Peter came to Him and said, "Lord, how many times shall I forgive my brother when he sins against me?" Peter understood that when going to your brother to tell him his fault, it was not going to accuse him, but rather to identify what he did that caused hurt so that you might forgive them. The keys here are to steer away from accusation and to become transparent.

The Importance of Transparency

Transparency is vital; you are going to let this person know that something they did or did not do caused a wound and you want to forgive them. As mentioned in a previous chapter, they might not even realize that they wounded you. Remember perception is important. You want to forgive them because of the way you perceived what they did that it caused you great hurt. Peter understood that when Jesus said, "go to your brother and tell him your fault," Jesus wasn't saying go to him and blame or accuse, rather Jesus was saying to him, "go to him to communicate forgiveness to him." When we place verse15 in context with the understanding of the disciples, we can see the truth of what Jesus was communicating.

Matthew 18:16 Jesus continues, "But if he will not listen, take one or two others along, so that every matter may be established by the testimony of two or three witnesses." Unfortunately, we misinterpreted this passage. We believe it means "Take with you one or two friends you have influenced by telling them in your own words what a terrible, heartless thing your brother did against you. Now they are on your side so you can gang up on your brother and prove you are right and he is wrong because three is always better than one!" So many of us live by this interpretation. However, I hate to break this to you, but that is not what Jesus is saying here. Jesus is about to teach the foundational principle of the power of unforgiveness and forgiveness: agreement. As Christians, agreement is a power that can be used for positive or negative effect. Jesus is about to lay it wide open. In verse 16 He tells us that when we include just one other in agreement, we have the authority of heaven behind us. "...every matter may be established by the testimony of two or three witnesses." Agreement is the fundamental undergirding principle to this whole thing of binding and loosing.

A Method of Recociliation

Romans 18:17, "If he refuses to listen to them, tell it to the church; and if he refuses to listen even to the church, treat him as you would a pagan or a tax collector." Unfortunately, this verse has brought about a lot of incorrect practice within the local church. Jesus is showing us here a method of reconciliation, rather than a method of church discipline which has been the focus of many leaders. Remember, this is a matter between two Christians. The progression so far has been, go by yourself; then if that fails to work, bring people with you. Throughout this process, the focus is always to bring about a reconciliation between two brothers (Christians). As I said previously, this process was never about proving yourself right and them wrong or pride and vengeance. I would like to note here the perseverance that is shown by the one who has been offended.

Unconditional love poured into our hearts by Jesus Christ can only explain this type of perseverance towards another. Only by love for one another, Jesus tells us in John 13:35, will the world see that we are different. Jesus is telling His disciples here to keep going back because unity, reconciliation, and love between Christians is a non-negotiable for us to be a credible witness to a world that needs Him. Now between each of these progressive steps is a refusal to hear, this is more than just mere negligence but rather an active refusal for reconciliation. Most of us will either give up here or take verse 16 as a time to take it to our church leaders. The Greek word here for church is *Ecclesia* which means assembly or congregation, not leadership or some hierarchal group. What Jesus wants here is for the power of agreement to spread to establish the ultimate goal, which is reconciliation between brothers. Tell it to the church so that now you have more than just two people who have witnessed your attempt at reconciliation within the relationship.

Now comes the most problematic part of this verse, ". . . and if he refuses to listen even to the church (Assembly), treat him as you would a pagan or a tax collector." So many people have been wounded, crushed and removed from the church (gathering) because of the misinterpretation of this verse. I want to point out that the context here is critical. Jesus is talking about an issue between two Christians. The actions of one Christian have hurt the other Christian. He has repeatedly gone to seek reconciliation with this brother, bringing along witnesses and finally involving a larger gathering of people to stand witness for him. After all this, there is still a refusal to reconcile. What must this brother do who has been offended? Notice, it is not what must the church, or church leadership do. This brother needs to treat him as a pagan, and tax collector. How do you treat pagans and tax collectors? I'll tell you how Jesus treated them, with compassion, love, and forgiveness, which drove the religious people nuts!

Matthew 11:19a, "The Son of Man came eating and drinking, and they say, 'Here is a glutton and a drunkard, a friend of tax collectors and sinners." So our root behavior and attitude towards them is still grounded in forgiveness, love, and compassion. I believe Jesus is saying here, "Still treat your brother with love and compassion and forgiveness, however as far as putting yourself in a place of receiving or fellowshipping with this brother guard your heart as you would with a pagan, be cautious lest you be wounded again!" It's all about expectation. What would you expect from a pagan or tax collector as a Jewish believer? You would expect them to act in non-Christian ways; therefore, your chance of getting offended and hurt by them is much lower than from a fellow Christian. Why, as a church, do we treat people within the church with less grace than we treat sinners?

The Authority We Have in Jesus

Matthew 18:18 - 20, now Jesus gets into the meat, "I tell you the truth, whatever you bind on earth will be bound in heaven, and whatever you loose on earth will be loosed in heaven. Again, I tell you that if two of you on earth agree about anything you ask for, it will be done for you by my Father in heaven. For where two or three come together in my name, there am I with them."

Within the history of the church, we had real problems in interpreting Matthew 18:18 – 20 because we tend to take these verses out of context and make them apply to things that Jesus was not primarily thinking of when he was teaching his disciples. What Jesus is speaking about in the whole context of Matthew 18 is on how we deal with offenses and for us, as Christians, to understand the kind of authority that we have in Jesus Christ. It is an authority that touches heaven and that when we decide on earth, we can move heaven by our decision. Jesus is not talking about a prayer meeting.

Many times verses 19 – 20 are quoted in the context of the local church coming together in a prayer meeting or worship service. Jesus is not talking about a prayer meeting or worship service. A good question to ask to put these verses in perspective is, "How many people do we have to have in a prayer meeting or worship time to have His presence with us?" The answer is "Only One" according to Romans 8:11." Jesus is talking about our authority in binding and loosing.

We find an excellent example of this type of agreement in 1 Corinthians 5. It's the story of a man who is in an incestuous relationship with his stepmother. The church acted like the situation wasn't a big issue. They did not deal with it and was rather proud and boastful about the whole situation. In this setting the Apostle Paul is writing to the church in Corinth, rebuking them for their attitude to this leaven that is leavening the whole lump (verse 6). In 1 Corinthians 5:4 – 5 Paul says this, "When you are assembled in the name of our Lord Jesus and I am with you in spirit and the power of our Lord Jesus is present, hand this man over to Satan, so that the sinful nature may be destroyed and his spirit saved on the day of the Lord." Here Paul is applying the principle that Jesus is talking about in Matthew 18:18 – 20. Paul is talking about authority in an agreed gathering of the church, whereby we come into agreement about a situation to bind or to loose a situation. When we do it in agreement, we have Jesus there to authenticate or back up our agreement. So what does this all mean practically for you and me?

One of the things that we love to do when someone else hurts us in the body of Christ is to make our gossip holy. What does that mean? When someone hurts us, it's not uncommon for us to pick up the telephone and share with people within our church. We tell them what has just happened and ask them to intercede and pray with us. Or better still, let's do it in person and have some coffee with friends while pouring out all our grievances, letting them know 'in love' how badly this so-called Christian has treated us. And oh, by the way, please pray for me. Sounds holy right, sounds Christian? What it doesn't sound like is what Jesus told us to do. "If your brother sins against you go and show him his fault, just between the two of you!" Why shouldn't I get prayer support? Why shouldn't I get my friends around me to help me? Because if you share it with one other person, you as two or more gathered together have now entered into an agreement which now releases the authority of heaven.

If you bring someone else into the unity of judgment with you against another Christian, you have just moved heaven into confirming your judgment. Now we have bound that Christian in heaven because as Christians we have the authority of Jesus to do so. When two members of the body of Christ come together in agreement over a situation heaven authenticates and backs up the agreement. That's why Jesus said, "Don't tell anyone else." You go to your brother and deal with the issue between you and him alone. If he doesn't listen to you, then you can take two witnesses, but remember they are just witnesses you have not contaminated with your story, nor given them all the juicy details. You need their witness, so if it comes before the larger assembly, they can relate that you have attempted a restoration with your brother, but he would not listen.

Paul in 1 Corinthians 5 is talking about members who have come together to agree on what to do with a brother. Because they come together in agreement, there is a power of binding and loosing released for the ultimate purpose of the restoration of someone who has fallen into a sinful act. As Christians, we don't need others to agree with us in prayer for God to answer us. He loves us; we are his children. We are as special to Him as Jesus is. We don't need others to come into agreement for God to give us what He has already promised us. Jesus here in Matthew 18:18 - 20 is talking about our authority when it comes to binding and loosing.

Keys of the Kingdom

In Matthew 16:18 – 19 Jesus introduces this concept to the church. He tells us, "And I tell you that you are Peter (*Petros* – little boulder), and on this rock (*Petra* – A large mass of rock) I will build my church, and the gates of Hades will not overcome it. I will give you the keys of the kingdom of heaven; whatever you bind on earth will be bound in heaven, and whatever you loose on earth will be loosed in heaven." First, the kingdom is built on the rock of revelation that the little boulder, Peter, uttered in Matthew 16:16. "Simon Peter answered, "You are the Christ, (Anointed One) the Son of the living God." The church is built and stands on the revelation that Jesus is the anointed one prophesied and is the true Son of God. Secondly, what are the keys of the kingdom? What are these keys that open up the door of the kingdom and the door of heaven for us? Forgiveness! How did we become children of God? By the true Son of God creating a way through His death and resurrection for us to be forgiven and reconciled to God so that we may be adopted into His family! One of the primary words for forgiveness is to loose!

The word "forgive" is the Greek word *aphiēmi*. It means to set free; to let go; to release; to discharge, or to liberate completely. It was used in a secular sense in New Testament times about canceling a debt or releasing someone from the obligation of a contract, a commitment, or promise. When God forgave us He loosed us from the bondage of the law, the bondage to keep all of the law to be acceptable before Him. When He forgave us because of the finished work of Jesus and Jesus canceling the effects of the law against us, he brought us to a place where the law had no more jurisdiction over us and where He freely forgave us. He forgave us not because we are a law keeper but because Jesus died for us! And so forgiveness is something us Christians are living in daily.

We are forgiven, and because we are forgiven we have been set free, and because we have been set free, we can experience what true life is all about. When God forgave us, His forgiveness opened up the door of heaven for all of us to come into His family! All this is spelled out in Ephesians 1:4 – 8, "For He chose us in Him before the creation of the world to be holy (set apart) and blameless in His sight in love he predestined us to be adopted as His sons through Jesus Christ, in accordance with His pleasure and will- to the praise of His glorious grace, which He has freely given us in the One He loves. In Him we have redemption through His blood, the forgiveness of sins, in accordance with the riches of God's grace that he lavished on us with all wisdom and under-standing."

In John 20:21 – 23, Jesus reveals a little more about the keys of the kingdom when talking to His disciples, "Peace be with you! As the Father has sent me, I am sending you." And with that, he breathed on them and said, "Receive the Holy Spirit. If you forgive anyone his sins, they are forgiven; if you do not forgive them, they are not forgiven."' Jesus breathed on them to receive the Spirit, and without any pause, He said, "If you forgive anyone his sins, they are forgiven; if you do not forgive them, they are retained." He is giving the keys to the kingdom to the disciples, as He told Peter He would. But He had to die first to wrest the keys from Satan. This event is taking place after Jesus has already died and risen from the grave and now He is telling His disciples, "Peace be with you." He's letting them know that peace has finally arrived. Why can they now have peace and why has it arrived? Peace has arrived because Jesus had died on the cross as a sacrifice for our sins. He then went up to the Father, who accepted His sacrifice. His blood was sprinkled on the mercy seat instead of lamb's blood which became a permanent cleansing of sin, and now there is peace.

The Father is no longer angry with us. Sin has been dealt with once and for all, and we have been forgiven. And now Jesus says, "Now get ready I'm going to breathe on you, you are going to receive the Holy Spirit, and have the anointing of heaven to use the keys of heaven. You can forgive sins, and when you forgive them they are forgiven, and when you retain them, they are retained. You now have the keys of the kingdom. I have wrenched them out of the hands of the devil, and I have given them to you. You can walk around, and you can release people and see them saved." The greatest hindrance to people being saved is unforgiveness. Maybe you have been praying for loved ones or family members for their salvation. Maybe this has been going on for years and years with no visible change. By this time, you have been wondering, "Will God ever save them?" Jesus, however, gave us a clue as to why so many people are still bound up within their prison. What He was telling us was that they are locked in a prison of unforgiveness.

Prisons of Unforgiveness

As Christians, we have cried, "God save my daughter, save my dad, my mom, my sister!" But God's reply will always be, "If you release them from the prison of unforgiveness you are holding them in I will save them in a flash. You have locked them in prison, but you have the keys to let them out!"

What you bind on earth you bind in heaven. The implication of this is when you bind others you get bound. When you lock others in prison, you get locked in a prison. If we don't exercise the grace that God has given us freely through Jesus, we are going to get judged with the same judgment that we give which results in us also getting locked up in prison.

This revelation is not easy to accept, but we need to know that God wants us to get out of these self-imposed prisons. He wants us to get out of the cells and the bondage of unforgiveness that ensnares us. He wants us to get out of these prisons so that we can stop binding others up through our mouths. We get ourselves into a whole stack of trouble because as soon as we are offended the first thing we do is go and tell someone else. When we do this, we have now gotten someone into an agreement with us, and then we wonder why God won't answer our prayers to change the situation.

You have used the keys that He gave you to bind them, and now you have brought someone into agreement with you, and as soon as you get someone into agreement with you, God confirms it in heaven. God has given us the keys of the kingdom. He gave us the power to forgive, but if we won't forgive and we bring someone into agreement with us to bind that person in the offense against us, He has to confirm it in heaven.

Fellow Christians, we need to understand that we have been given the authority to bind and to loose, to release or to retain, to condemn or to release others from condemnation. We have been given the keys to His Kingdom, and it's an amazing responsibility for us to use in conjunction with the grace that He has lavished on us so that we can lavish the same grace on others, even though we think they don't deserve it. We can turn them loose anytime

we wish and let God then do what He wants to do which is to reconcile them to Himself!

A few years ago, a friend of mine and His wife were going
through a separation and a divorce. They were separated for
months due to infidelity. Through this process, God revealed
Himself to my friend, and he had an amazing encounter with God
while alone in the apartment that he was now staying in because
he was separated from his children and his spouse. God met him,
someone who was an agnostic, and while alone he had an amazing
salvation experience. Suddenly, whereas before he had no desire
to reunite with his wife God changed his heart, and he once again
desired to have her back. However, his wife was not interested in
taking him back. During a lunch break, while I was facilitating a
seminar in Minneapolis Minnesota, he had called me, battling
with the facts that he and his wife might never reconcile. During
our conversation, I went through the *talk* and *walk* of forgiveness
with him. He released his wife from what he had perceived as her
wrongdoings.

The next day he called me all excited. His wife had called him
and asked him to come back home. He had released her from that
prison and in so doing released himself and their relationship.
The story with my friend and his wife did not end there. His and
her walk in forgiveness has been a long one, a few more separa-
tions, and learning for both of them in the lessons of binding and
loosing. In the process of this walk of forgiveness, his wife came
to know Christ as he continued to release her from the prison he
created for her. He has been set free from a sexual addiction that
had held him for years as she learned to release him from the
prison she created for him. I have sometimes watched from a distance, and sometimes from close by as I've counseled and lavished

grace on both of them, the freedom that forgiveness has brought them in their relationship.

God has given to us in the church the keys of the kingdom, and unfortunately, we haven't done a good job in exercising the keys of the kingdom. God's greatest desire is for the church to start forgiving, for the church to start exercising that key of forgiveness. Jesus tells us that we have His authority and we have His power. We have His discernment to go to people and say, "You're forgiven," but He also says that "Whoever sins you shall retain shall be retained." We have these keys. Let us release others!

As the church, we could shut down abortion clinics tomorrow if we just went and stood outside and started using the keys of the kingdom by releasing the forgiveness of God on the abortionists and the woman that were entering those clinics. Instead, the church is standing outside with their banners, and we are getting angry and hostile, screaming condemnation. As Christians we are not given a ministry of confrontation; we were committed to a ministry of reconciliation. "All this is from God, who reconciled us to Himself through Christ and gave us the ministry of reconciliation:" 2 Corinthians 5:18 What the church should be doing is standing outside abortion clinics telling those who are entering that, ". . . that God is reconciling the world to Himself in Christ, not counting men's sins against them." 2 Corinthians 5:19. And according to the second part of verse 19 through 20, "And He has committed to us the message of reconciliation. We are therefore Christ's ambassadors, as though God were making His appeal through us." But what we are telling them is, "God's going to get you! God is going to judge you!" That's not the gospel. The good news of the gospel is found in verse 20 and 21.

First, our hearts should be that of an immense desire to see them reconciled to Him and not judged. "We implore you on Christ's behalf: Be reconciled to God." Second, we now see the good news, "God made Him who had no sin to be sin for us, so that in Him we might become the righteousness of God." In other words, Christ wants to change their position, from a position of separation to one of right standing in God's sight!

Bound in Condemnation

What we are doing, however, is binding them up in condemnation and judgment. God is asking us, what do you want me to do? Do you want me to change them, or judge them? Our message to the world sometimes can be so confusing. We scream judgment with more glee than we call for reconciliation. As the church, we need to start loosing them and watching God change their situation. The tongue is what we are using to destroy the work of God in the church of Jesus Christ. The tongue has been used to destroy what God wants to do in the earth. Our tongues have been used to allow the enemy to set ablaze a deadly fire of destruction within our churches, our marriages, our families.

We wonder why we are so bound up. No wonder our finances are in the mess they are in, or why we are not getting the healing that we have been praying for from God. He is telling us that we are in prison because we've locked others in prison.

In the story of the unforgiving servant in Matthew 18: 23 - 35 we see this scenario play out. After the King had demanded that the man who owed the debts family be sold we see in verse 26, "The servant fell on his knees before Him. 'Be patient with me,' he begged, 'and I will pay back everything.'" In verse 27, "The servant's master took pity on him, canceled the debt and let him go." The master loosed him (This is the same Greek word used in Matthew 16:19, "whatever you loose on earth will be loosed in heaven.") and forgave his debt. But now he goes and finds someone else to bind up.

I wonder if this sounds like something we have done before? God forgives us freely all our sin, and then one day we go and hold something against someone else because of something they did which is the same thing this servant did in Matthew 18:30. "But he refused." He refused to do what? To loose! "Instead, he went off and had the man thrown into prison until he could pay the debt." I would like to point out two things here: (1) He bound him in prison and (2) He cut off the man's ability to pay the debt back.

Our refusal to forgive not only binds people in prison but severs their ability to pay us back, which if we follow the logic leaves them in that prison indefinitely.

So, what happens to this servant who would not forgive and loose his fellow servant? In Matthew 18:32 – 35, Jesus continues, "Then the master called the servant in, 'You wicked servant,' He said, 'I canceled all that debt of yours because you begged me to. Shouldn't you have had mercy on your fellow servant just as I had on you? In anger his Master turned him over to the jailers to be tortured, until he should pay back all he owed. This is how my Heavenly Father will treat each of you unless you forgive your brother from your heart.'"

The Power of Forgiveness

John Sheasby tells an amazing story of a lady that he visited who was dying of cancer. The doctors had given her two weeks to live. John prayed for her, and he admits to it being a 'religious prayer over her' expecting not much to happen and then he had left. The next day while he was out jogging, God had started to speak to him. John relates that God had told him that this lady had cancer and was blind because of unforgiveness and that if he would go to her and talk to her about forgiveness and help her to forgive, He would heal her! John went to see her the very next day and when he walked in immediately told her that God was going to heal her that very day if she would forgive.

What John found out was that this lady was conceived illegitimately. Her parents did not want her, and so she was placed in an institution where she grew up for the first five to six years of her life. From there she was fostered, and her foster parents decided to adopt her eventually. The sad thing was that her adopted mother hated her because her adoptive father loved her. The mother was so jealous of all the affection that the adoptive father was giving to this little girl that she became very abusive to her secretly. She would abuse her by beating her and using other physical and verbal methods of abuse. She went through a whole life of sexual perversion and abuse and four separate abusive marriages, until finally ending up blind, alone with cancer and dying.

After the lady finished her story, John began teaching her about forgiveness, about how she could be set free from the prison that she found herself in and how to be free from the torturers. John led her through forgiveness, forgiving everyone from her parents who had conceived her but abandoned her, to forgiving the terrible things that happened to her in the orphanage. She forgave the adoptive mother that abused and mistreated her. She forgave the men and husbands that had physically and sexually abused and abandoned her. Once the talk of forgiveness was complete, John let her know that the Lord wanted to heal her of all the wounds that had been inflicted upon her.

The Holy Spirit then took her back to various memories of her life, especially one of them. This one memory was one of the most powerful. When she was only four years of age, she had contracted an infectious disease, so the matrons in the orphanage had isolated her and placed her in a room separated from the other children. She was so isolated that she would not see anyone else except at meal times when they would bring her meals. One day, as she was in this room, locked away, and in loneliness and isolation, a few children stood at the door of her room. They began to tease her and told her that she was never coming out of that room ever again. At that moment her little four-year-old heart was broken in two, and in her perception, she felt shut out and abandoned. A deep emotional wound scared her heart.

As John sat with her, he began to pray and invite Jesus to come into that situation and reveal the truth. In her memory, she saw Jesus walk into that isolated room and pick up her four-year-old self and hold her in His arms. At that moment John said that the lady started to speak like that four-year-old little girl as she responded to the love of Jesus for the first time. She was immediately healed emotionally. John then began to pray for her physical healing, and when they were done she opened her eyes and said, "I can see you!" That night she got out of bed and went to the church where John was ministering, totally healed! The tormentor had left her; she had been loosed from her prison as she released others from theirs.

I believe the reason why a lot of people are not getting saved is that we have not dealt with the bitterness and the unforgiveness and the binding that we have done towards them. We have bound people in our unforgiveness out of our wounds, and then we come to God and ask Him to heal us. God wants to heal us because healing is part of our inheritance, healing is our birthright, but because of our unforgiveness, we've put ourselves in prison by binding others inside a prison.

I would like to relate one more story that John Sheasby tells that perfectly illustrates this binding and loosing principle. John was preaching in a church in Florida where a lady approached him after the Monday morning lunchtime service. She told John that she had been depressed for the last eight years and she could find no way out of this depression. She was a Spirit-filled Christian but was in a state of constant depression. Her husband was a pilot in Vietnam and went missing in action during the Vietnam War, and for years she and the family had heard no news about how and where or if he was dead. Then eight years ago the military authorities contacted her husband's parents and told them there was some news coming about MIA's from Vietnam. The problem was that her husband's parents never contacted her to let her know about the news. She was contacted two days later by the military authorities to let her know.

When this lady found out that the authorities had spoken to her husband's parents and his parents had never bothered to contact her, a rage erupted within her against them, especially her mother-in-law. Her mother-in-law had been against the marriage from the beginning, and according to this lady, she didn't like her, wouldn't receive her and never received her as a daughter-in-law. There had always been tension under the surface between them. When her mother-in-law failed to contact her about her husband, this action was the straw that broke the camel's back. This behavior pushed her over the edge, and she spent the next two years institutionalized with the severest of depression.

After two years, she was released from the institution and decided to move from California across the United States to Florida thinking that she could start her life over again. She moved from California to Florida, thinking that she had left her past behind, but she carried the depression with her. She lived with this depression night and day, never being set free from its effects. At that meeting, John started talking to her about the freedom of forgiveness, showing her the power of what we have been talking about in this book. Her response is what everybody we ever talk to about forgiveness and share what the Word of God teaches about forgiveness: "But what if I had to forgive her! How will she respond?" Suddenly fear raised its head. Let me pause right here and quickly deal with this type of objection.

When the Holy Spirit begins to prompt us about the need to forgive, our mind starts to turn towards future scenarios. We start to think of what might or might not happen if we had to listen to what the Word says for us to do. We need to recognize what these thoughts are and where they originate. They are purely speculative thoughts. We think that if we forgive, the response to that forgiveness might be incredibly negative. We say to ourselves, "Well they might do this, and this might result, and this might happen. And if I forgive them, they might come back into my life, and they will mess me up like they messed me up before. They could take advantage of my forgiveness and keep hurting me, etc."

A speculative thought is a manifestation of a spirit of fear. In 2 Timothy 1:7, the Bible tells us that, "For God has not given us a spirit of fear, but of love, power and a *sound* mind." (My emphasis added.) So if you are having speculative thoughts, you need to know that there is a spirit of fear beneath them. So the question must then be if you have a spirit of fear from where does it originate? The answer to a Christian is simple, the enemy. So why does Satan put the spirit of fear inside you? He desires to keep you locked up in your self-imposed prison of unforgiveness. He doesn't want you to get out of that prison because he loves you being locked up and tortured. He knows that as long as you are in prison, he can steal all of your inheritance. He can devour your marriage, he can devour your children, and he can steal your finances. Guess what he has come to do? To steal, kill and destroy! So as long as you are in prison, he is very happy. The moment you start thinking about forgiving someone he starts getting nervous, and when you start taking the steps, he is the one who begins to fear. If you want to be free of the torturers and free from the prison you are in and especially free from the enemy tormenting you with fear, you need to forgive.

When this lady went down the road of speculation and fear, John let her know that it was not important how her mother-in-law responded to her. The most important part was that if she wanted to be free from this depression, free from this tormentor that was upon her, she needed to forgive. According to her if she called her mother-in-law, she was going to give her a positive thinking seminar because she was in a cult that denies everything negative and only positive thoughts are allowed. All this didn't matter. What mattered was whether she was going to forgive her mother-in-law or not. What mattered was whether she was going to take a step towards the talk and finally the walk of forgiveness or not. "Will you do it?" was all John asked her. After some reluctance and convincing from the Word of God, she finally agreed that she would do it.

She went home and was still very reluctant to do it, so she waited until 3:40 pm that afternoon. Finally, she called her mother-in-law and told her that she wanted to forgive her and got the reaction she had expected and had been dreading. Now if the story ends here, it would be a good story, but that would be all. Twenty minutes later her telephone rang, and when she answered, it was her mother-in-law on the other end. The first words she heard were, " I don't understand what's happened to me. I've been running around, skipping and dancing like a little child. I feel like a bird released from its cage! I feel like I have just been let out of a prison." Remember, this woman's mother-in-law was an unsaved woman who was in a cult. She had nothing to do with Christianity nor the Bible, yet she was feeling the effects of what Jesus was teaching when He said, "What you bind on earth is bound in heaven, what you loose on earth is loosed in heaven."

The end of John's story gives me goosebumps because it illustrates so well what we have been talking about in this chapter and, in fact, throughout this entire book. When John went to preach at that church sometime later, this lady told him the follow-up story. Shortly after she forgave her mother-in-law, she had the privilege to lead her mother-in-law to Jesus. The relationship between the lady and her mother-in-law was made new to the point where they have become the best of friends. Through her ministering inner healing by the Holy Spirit to her mother-in-law, she has been healed of all of her past hurts.

As Christians, we need to grasp that we have the keys of the kingdom. We have this power because the Holy Spirit has given it to us. However, the problem is we threw away the keys and began to agree with the Pharisees who said to Jesus, "Who can forgive sins but God!" It's such a powerful thing to watch when we tell someone that we forgive them and we tell them that their sins are forgiven as immediately the freedom of Christ comes within them. We have the authority, we have been given the keys, and we need to exercise that authority under the power of the Holy Spirit. We need to hear and be led by the Spirit.

Some of you are experiencing the effects of taking the keys of the kingdom and choosing not to use them, choosing not to release others from their prisons, choosing to hold against them what they have done. You have said in your hearts, "I'm not going to unlock the prison. They don't deserve it, and I won't do it!" When you choose to do this because hopefully as you have read this book, you realize by now that this is a personal choice, the Holy Spirit wants to remind you that there is a principle that will begin to work in you, called sowing and reaping. And He is saying to you now, "What you sow you reap!"

I want to finish this chapter with the words of Jesus from the book of Luke. In Luke 6:30 – 38 Jesus speaking to the crowds said these words, "Give to everyone who asks you, and if anyone takes what belongs to you, do not demand it back. Do to others as you would have them do to you. If you love those who love you, what credit is that to you? Even 'sinners' love those who love them. And if you do good to those who are good to you, what credit is that to you? Even 'sinners' do that. And if you lend to those from whom you expect repayment, what credit is that to you? Even 'sinners' lend to a 'sinner,' expecting to be repaid in full. But love your enemies, do good to them, and lend to them without expecting to get anything back. Then your reward will be great, and you will be sons of the Most High, because He is kind to the ungrateful and wicked. Be merciful, just as your Father is merciful. Do not judge, and you will not be judged. Do not condemn and you will not be condemned. Forgive, and you will be forgiven. Give and it will be given to you. A good measure, pressed down, shaken together and running over, will be poured into your lap. For with the measure you use, it will be measured to you."

It is time for you to release them and let them go!

CHAPTER SEVENTEEN

Release Them and Let Them Go!

"Then Peter came to Jesus and asked, "Lord, how many times shall I forgive my brother when he sins against me? Up to seven times? "Jesus answered, "I tell you, not seven times, but seventy-seven times." Matthew 18:21-22 (NIV)

In Hollywood, some of the most popular movies from the past and present are those movies that require the hero of the story to extract revenge. The 'bad guy' commits an injustice. We cheer, we applaud, and we feel vindicated when the 'bad guy' gets put in his place. Sometimes the more gruesome that payback is, the more satisfied we feel. For most of us we would not get payback in that way, but without realizing it, many of us project our anger and frustration regarding the wrongs we have experienced onto the big screen; consequently, we also experience the joy of revenge through the eyes of the hero on that screen.

When Peter approached Jesus in Matthew 18:21, he honestly wanted to know the forgiveness limit. He wanted to know what he needed to put up with others misdeeds towards him. Within the Jewish rabbinical teachings of the law, the follower of the law was only required to forgive up to three times. When they had forgiven the three times required by law, and the person continued to do what they had forgiven them for, a law-abiding Jew had every right to seek revenge. The teaching of the Rabbis was only three, so when Peter said to Jesus, seven times he was going way beyond the teaching of the Rabbis and the traditions of the fathers. Jesus replied, "I tell you, not seven times, but seventy-seven times." I can imagine the look on Peter's face. Here he is thinking that he was showing how forgiving and obedient he is and then Jesus takes it to a whole new level which left the teaching of the Rabbis in the dust. After Jesus responded to Peter, he then tells an incredible story. We touched on the story briefly in our last chapter, but it is one that needs to be looked at a little more closely. The story is about a king who had servants indebted to him, and he needed to settle their accounts.

In Matthew 18:23 – 27 Jesus begins the story, "Therefore, the kingdom of heaven is like a king who wanted to settle accounts with his servants. As he began the settlement, a man who owed him ten thousand talents (millions of dollars in our currency) was brought to him. Since he was not able to pay, the master ordered he and his wife and his children and all that he had be sold to repay the debt. The servant fell on his knees before him. 'Be patient with me,' he begged, 'and I will pay back everything.' The servant's master took pity on him, canceled the debt and let him go." I mentioned this in the previous chapter, but I need to reiterate it because it is that important. When you and I release others with the keys of the kingdom that Jesus' has given to us, we open their prisons. We also open our prison doors with the key we used to let others out of prison.

Releasing is one of the most important things that Christians and the church of Jesus need to understand. The key to the kingdom is the key of forgiveness. When we unlock a door with the key of forgiveness, there is a loosing that goes on in heaven that releases God's power into the situation. Many times, we are praying for people through one side of our mouths, and from the other side we are binding them up, then we wonder why God never answers our prayers and saves them. In James 3:10, James tells us, "Out of the same mouth come praise and cursing. My brothers, this should not be. Can both fresh water and salt water flow from the same spring? My brothers, can a fig tree bear olives, or a grapevine bear figs? Neither can a salt spring produce fresh water." God is letting us know that if we would only let them go and loose them out of their prison that He would go after them in a hurry.

In Matthew 18:27 Jesus uses the Greek word, *aphēken*. The verb is *aphiēmi* pronounced *af-ee-ay-mee*, and in its simplest form means to forgive, but it means so much more as we will see. The word '*aphiēmi*' is a legal term. It's a word used in Jesus' time for the cancellation of any debt owed, but not only was it used for the debt of money, but it was the word also used for divorce. When a couple went through a divorce, and they came to sign the legal document releasing them from the marriage, that legal document became an '*aphiēmi*.' This word meant the releasing of the person from all previously binding obligations under a previous contract of marriage, business, debt or anything else they were obligated to fulfill. So, when a Jew gave somebody an '*aphiēmi*' or 'a forgiveness,' they were releasing them from the need to fulfill an obligation. As Christians, it is essential that we understand the significance of this amazing word. The word '*aphiēmi*' and the equivalent word in Hebrew is the most commonly used word for forgiveness in the Bible. What can we derive from this word and its meaning?

Forgiveness is not an emotion. What confuses us most about forgiveness is the idea that forgiveness is an emotion. When we have heard a message or read a book on forgiveness, and we come face to face with the truth that we might need to forgive someone, we examine our emotions to feel whether we have any resentment, or bitterness, or even anger. When we find nothing, which tends to be the case in most instances, unless some hurt has happened recently, we push it aside and tell ourselves or the person who has asked us, "No, I don't have anything to forgive!" Unforgiveness has nothing to do with the way you feel.

Unforgiveness is a matter of keeping an uncanceled record of something that somebody did to you. You might even have uttered the words, "I forgive them" but you still vividly remember what they did, and their action still sits squarely in your mind. What this is telling you is that you have not canceled the debt out of the records. You are still holding on to unforgiveness, and you have not applied '*aphiēmi*.'

Canceled Records

What true forgiveness means is that whatever wounded you has now been canceled entirely out of the records. You do not have that event or series of events on your mind any longer. All this is possible because God showed us that it is possible by forgiving us in that way. In Psalm 103:12 the word tells us that, "as far as the east is from the west, so far has he removed our transgression from us." And again in Hebrews 8:12, "For I will forgive their wickedness and will remember their sins no more." This type of forgiveness is only possible by the power of the Holy Spirit and through the compassion of Jesus released in you and me. We will talk in more detail about His compassion in the next chapter.

It is possible to get to the place where that which was once a painful experience recorded in your ledger is canceled. The very experience of one of the four weapons used against you, and for which you are expecting payback or satisfaction, can be canceled in your ledger. When you remember that experience, you remember it without any negative feeling. In fact, when the Holy Spirit has done His whole work in you, you can remember that once painful experience with joy because you can see the full blessing of God that came because of that experience. God wants to and does redeem every situation. He redeems that which could be potentially devastating and a huge stumbling block for you and turns it into a stepping stone in your spiritual life.

A lot of people I talk to think they have forgiven because they don't feel bad about the situation anymore. Remember emotions and feelings are not the guides as to whether you have forgiven or not. They can be powerful indicators that there is unforgiveness, but on the other side, they can also be a distractor to what is really going on inside. So, you're probably asking, "Orrin, if I can't depend on my feelings as an indicator of unforgiveness, what can I depend on? How can I know that I have unforgiveness? How can I know that I have not yet canceled the debt?" Here are a few indicators that will help you in this regard.

Signs the Debt is Not Canceled
Debt Collectors

We become debt collectors. Just like the man in Matthew 18:28, "But when the servant went out, he found one of his fellow servants who owed him a hundred denarii. He grabbed him and began to choke him. Pay back what you owe me! He demanded." You begin to make others pay the debt the original person owes you. The sad thing is that when we still have debt on our ledger, we go around choking everyone around us for payment of that debt.

My first position in ministry, after I finished Bible college was in a church in East London, South Africa. I was involved with a ministry called J.O.T. (Jesus our Teacher). The church hired me as a youth pastor within the church, but part of my ministry was to also work for the local high schools as a free teacher. The J.O.T teachers would coach sports, become one of the school counselors, teach Bible Education and take on the responsibilities of a full-time teacher. During the time I was teaching, I was also co-running our church youth group. Our youth group in the church grew exponentially, and most of the growth came from the kids I was teaching in the local high schools.

The senior pastor recognized the impact that I was having on the youth group and the growth of his church because many of the parents of those children started attending. He met with me at his home and told me not to let anyone else know about the meeting, especially the leader of the J.O.T. ministry. He mentioned that he was looking to promote me to an assistant pastor within the church and that I should not let the J.O.T. head know because he was also looking for this promotion. He also mentioned that I had shown my worth and was the obvious choice. As a young man fresh in ministry being a pastor was what I had studied for, and it was what people who are called to ministry by God were 'meant to be;' it was my dream.

What I did not realize back then was that I was title chasing. I was looking for acknowledgment, recognition, and status because I had this huge empty void within that had never been filled in childhood. I always felt I needed to prove myself to be accepted, to be the best, to be on top. So, when this pastor promised me this position, I was elated. About a year later, the man who was over the J.O.T. ministry was promoted to the position promised to me. I felt he was reaping all the honors for the youth growing, even though two-thirds of the youth group were kids from the school where I was teaching. Yes. He was promoted instead of me, even though in that meeting the pastor promised me that would not happen. I was devastated, hurt, angry and resentful towards both of these men.

Now here is the sad part of this story. From then on, every pastor that I worked for I viewed with suspicion. I expected them to lie to me, hurt me, and make promises they never fulfilled. I was not disappointed. Many of them did exactly what I was expecting. My ministry life became a self-fulfilling prophecy. I was demanding these other pastors to pay a debt that they had not incurred, and that they could not pay. It left me frustrated in ministry and functionally depressed. My so-called results started to fall away, and I was almost fired from two ministry positions and was fired from one.

I was going around collecting debts. I viewed anyone who reminded me of the previous situation with suspicion. I had become a debt collector, and it was destroying me from the inside out. Here is another sad truth: debt collecting can propel you into situations where you are vulnerable to pick up more and more debts that you need to collect. You become a professional debt collector. As in my case, I was collecting the debt from that pastor to pay the need for acceptance that I was so longing to receive from my father. So, anyone in authority in my life owed me that debt. In turn, because the debt from my father remained unpaid, I started collecting the next level of debt that the pastor had created by not fulfilling the first debt. And so, the cycle repeats and grows.

There are a lot of people sitting in churches collecting debts from their present pastor because they are judging them against the backdrop of a past pastor who didn't do what they expected him to do. Over the years I've watched pastors who've had people join their church, and these people are mad that some previous pastor failed them. They come into this new church with all their expectations on their new leader. They want him to meet all their needs, or they will go to the next church. Someone once said to me, "The way you leave something is the way you enter the next thing." In other words, if you leave mad, you will enter mad. I was leaving one ministry that would not pay my debt and entering another one expecting them to pay it. I had not learned to forgive, so I held others in debt.

We see this in marriages. A wife who suffered sexual abuse as a child—her father might be the abuser—and as time goes by she can block out that memory and get to a place where she can have a good relationship with her father despite the abuse. But when it comes to her husband and giving herself unreservedly to him, she cannot. She is making her husband pay the debt that her father owes her. Debt collecting will show you whether you have indeed forgiven or not. You push things down, and you push things back, but you will keep collecting debts. This collection process is the first sign that you haven't canceled the original debt.

Lack of Compassion

In Matthew 18:27, "The servant's master took pity on him, canceled the debt and let him go." The Greek word used here for pity is the word, '*splanchnistheis*' which means a deep feeling of compassion. When you think of the person who hurt you 'if' you have forgiven him or her then when you see the person's face coming before you compassion will flow out of your innermost being toward them. You see, the Lord of the servant forgave with the release of compassion.

Unfortunately, when you are operating in unforgiveness, to be able to imagine a situation where you could feel compassion for the person who hurt you is impossible. Unforgiveness is a blockage to the flow of compassion. So, when you answer a probing question like, "Can you be around the person who hurt you?" with a resounding "No, it would be torturous!" then you haven't truly forgiven. You might have talked the talk but, somewhere in the walk of forgiveness, you picked up the judge's gavel again. You might have forgiven in your head, but you haven't forgiven from your heart."

The release of compassion is one of the most accurate demonstrations of true forgiveness. One of the signs of that release of compassion is in our ability to give to others. In 1 John 3:17 John tells us, "If anyone has material possessions and sees a brother or sister in need but has no pity on them, how can the love of God be in that person?" In the original Greek, this passage reads, "If anyone who has the goods of the world sees a brother of him in need, shuts off his deep emotions towards him, how can the love of God abide in him?" The phrase 'shuts up or closes off' denotes a choice by the one who is doing the shutting off.

We see this all the time among people who were told by their parents that struggle was good for them. When they first got married (although their parents had the resources to help them) they left them on their own to struggle and scrape by and have an incredibly hard time. Now, as parents, they say the same thing to their children, "It's good for you to struggle." You are making your children pay the stupid debt that your parents owe you for having closed their bowels of compassion because their parents did the same thing to them.

What kind of Christianity do we have where we have parents that have plenty of money, their kids get married, and the parents watch while the children struggle to make ends meet? Where did we get that insane idea from and where do we find this principle in the word of God?" What we have done is take the traditions of men and place them above God's word. We are making our children pay a debt that was owed to us by our parents. We have not forgiven our parents for making us struggle, and now we are making our children pay our debt. The Father's heart is to bless His children at the expense of His own needs going unmet.

Why do we have such crazy ideas that we need our children to struggle through life and think that is good for them? When we have the compassion of Jesus in us and flowing through us, we can't help becoming a giver to those around us. Giving is an indicator that you are living in forgiveness. Like Jesus, we will start giving to those who wrong us; we will start giving to those who hurt us, and we will keep on giving.

Unforgiveness blocks the true heart of the Father and holds us back from us manifesting His DNA which is in us since Christ dwells in us. Conversely, forgiveness releases that DNA to become evident to the world, even those who wrong us, and will let the world know that we are truly His disciples. One of the most potent ways to show love is to give from a heart of compassion.

Let's talk about how many Christians within the body of Christ go about canceling debt. Here I want to use an illustration to show the way we have acted in the church and some of the teaching that has come into being.

Bill and Mike

A man in the church, let's call him Bill, is in financial need. He wants to add extensions to the family house. So, Bill starts looking for a wealthy person within the church he is attending to help him out. He finds the person, we will call him Mike, and goes to Mike and asks him for a loan for the construction that he wants to do. Mike thinks about it for a bit and tells Bill that he has about $50,000 that he is not using now. So, Mike loans Bill the $50,000. In this process and due to the compassion within Mike for Bill's plight, he tells Bill that he will not charge him any interest on the money and that Bill can pay back the money when he is ready. He assures Bill that there is no rush.

Well, time goes on, Bill completes the construction, and weeks then months go by without any payment or attempted payment on the loan. Now during this time, Bill buys a new car. Mike starts thinking, "You know, Bill hasn't paid me back any of the money he owes me, but he sure is starting to spend a lot of money." A small emotional crack starts to develop between Mike and Bill. Every time Mike comes to church and sees Bill standing a few pews ahead of him in church with hands raised in worship to God, Mike starts to get a little annoyed and even angry. In fact, worship time in church is no longer enjoyable for Mike, because all he is doing is looking at Bill's new car and the new clothes that he and his family are wearing. All of this is making Mike more and more angry with Bill.

One day, however, the pastor preaches a powerful message on restoring relationships with your fellow Christians, and Mike feels convicted of holding all these feelings and bad attitudes towards Bill. So, after church, Mike calls Bill over and asks him to forgive him for the bad attitude that he has had against him. Of course, Bill with much gusto tells Mike that he will forgive him. They hug, they shake hands, they might even shed a tear, all is forgiven. Man, it feels great, the relationship has been sorted out!

Two weeks later, Bill takes his wife on a trip to Hawaii for their anniversary. Mike gets hit with another emotional thought: "Hang on, Bill still hasn't paid me any of the money he owes me, and here he is off to Hawaii with my money!" Suddenly all the feelings that he thought he dealt with come rushing back. The problem with Mike is that he never did anything with the original debt, he just dealt with his reaction.

Unfortunately, this is the way a lot of people deal with unforgiveness. There is an original hurt but rather than confront the situation they go to the person they have unforgiveness towards and apologize for the bad attitude or feelings of anger they have against that person. You find that this is the way many children deal with resentment towards their parents. Instead of going to deal with the original issue that hurt them they go to their parents and ask them for forgiveness for being rebellious or having been a bad kid and not having shown their parents respect or the love that they deserved, etc. And of course, the parents who are now thinking, "Finally they are getting it!" tell their children, "Of course, I forgive you!" but this has not resolved the situation at all. The children will still be debt collectors in their marriages and families, and the cycle will continue until they have dealt with the original debt.

Let's continue with the illustration. One day Mike is sitting in church again, and his pastor preaches another message, this time about forgiving the debt. He feels led by the Spirit that if he truly wants to get out of this cycle of anger, frustration and brooding he needs to write off the debt. He needs to cancel the debt once and for all. So, after church, he goes up to his pastor and tells his pastor that he has decided to cancel the debt against Bill for the $50,000! The pastor looks at Mike and says, "Okay, that is great, but why are you telling me?" "Well," Mike says, "I just wanted you to know what I am doing!" The pastor looks at Mike and says, "That's wonderful, but why are you telling me? If your brother sins against you, go to your brother and tell him his fault between you and him alone!"

There is no surrogate forgiveness. Going to God and telling him that you have forgiven the person that has wronged you, doesn't deal with that debt according to what God's word tells us. The Father is going to say to you as Jesus said in Matthew 5:23-24, "Therefore, if you are offering your gift at the altar and there remember that your brother has something against you, leave your gift there in front of the altar. First go and be reconciled to your brother; then come and offer your gift." Jesus wasn't just offering some good advice; there was a significant reason that he said what he said. If you keep reading, you find out why. Jesus continues in Matthew 5:25-26, "Settle matters quickly with your adversary who is taking you to court. Do it while you are still with him on the way, or he may hand you over to the judge, and the judge may hand you over to the officer, and you may be thrown into prison. I tell you the truth, you will not get out until you have paid the last penny."

When we come before God in worship but have a judgment against somebody, we set ourselves up as a judge under the law. Then according to what James tells us in James 2:10, "For whoever keeps the whole law and yet stumbles at just one point is guilty of breaking all of it." The law is not something that we can pick and choose the part we should obey or not obey. If we choose to live by law, according to James, then we are obligated to keep all of the law.

When we come before God with judgment in our hearts, we do not approach a throne of grace but a throne of judgment. God now becomes a judge towards us because we have become judges and issued judgment against another individual. We're not walking in grace, so God cannot show grace toward us. Through choosing to become judges, we have chosen how we would like God to relate to us, and the basis we chose is judgment. We said in our hearts, "God I have chosen to judge another person," and so in reply to our free choice He says, "You will get the judgment that you have chosen to give." The method by which you judge is the method by which you are judged. In Matthew 7:1, Jesus tells us just that, "Do not judge, or you too will be judged. For in the same way you judge others, you will be judged, and with the measure you use, it will be measured to you."

We move out of grace when we have a judgment. When we come before God in worship and tell Him that we love Him, God looks at the judgment in our heart for someone else and sees that we are lying. And just as Jesus said in Matthew 5:25, ". . . he may hand you over to the judge, and the judge may hand you over to the officer, and you may be thrown into prison." In other translations, it says, "Hand you over to be tortured." We are speaking against one another, holding grudges, judgments and unforgiveness and we wonder why we are coming to God in prayer, and our prayers go unanswered. The reason is we are not coming to a throne of grace as Hebrews 4:16 tells us, "Let us then approach the throne of grace with confidence, so that we may receive mercy and find grace to help us in our time of need." We come looking for mercy and help yet we are not willing to show mercy or give help to others in their need because we have judged them based on their behaviors, and actions. We want God to ignore our behaviors and actions towards Him so that we might receive the mercy that we are unwilling to give.

We are now no longer approaching that throne of grace, but rather we are now coming to a throne of judgment because we have judgment. God has now become our judge. He did not choose this for us, Jesus took all judgment on the cross of Calvary, yet we have chosen through our judgments to receive judgment again. That is why Jesus told us not to go to God if our brother sins against us but go to that individual and tell him his fault, between him and us alone. Let us not get heaven involved. Because of what we learned in the previous chapter: whatever you bind on earth is bound in heaven, don't let it go further than one on one or otherwise what you bind on earth is bound in heaven.

Unfortunately, many preachers and teachers who have not been willing to deal with unforgiveness in their own lives are not willing to teach us about what we must do when we have unforgiveness in our lives. They have watered down God's word when it comes to unforgiveness and judgment, because not only are they holding unforgiveness towards others, but also, they love to preach judgment from their pulpits towards those that are not living up to their standards. They are standing before a throne of judgment, and it is torturing them.

We have heard the saying, "Misery loves company," and unfortunately there are a lot of preachers and Christians who deep down are miserable because instead of experiencing God's grace and mercy daily, all they are experiencing is His judgment, because of their choice. They are miserable, and they don't want to be miserable alone. They will not preach grace and mercy nor the power of true forgiveness. Why? Because "I'm not willing to do that. I'm not willing to go to those who've offended me, nor am I willing to stop judging others. So, I'm going to water down what the word says so that it fits my agenda!" Remember, God's purpose is always reconciliation and restoration of relationship. As Jesus so aptly put it, "A new command I give you: Love one another, as I have loved you, so you must love one another. By this all men will know that you are my disciples, if you love one another." John 13:34 – 35.

One of the ways that we show this love to others is to cover them. In the Hebrew, there is a word used for forgiveness that means 'to cover.' It's an Old Testament word used to mean when you forgive somebody you cover that person's offense. In the New Testament, the Greek does not have an equivalent word, but in the story of Peter and his denial of Christ, you see this word in action by the way Jesus deals with Peter.

We all know the story of Peter found in the 26th chapter of Matthew. Jesus reveals to His disciples that they will abandon Him in Matthew 26:31, "Then Jesus told them, "This very night you will all fall away on account of me..." Peter said to Jesus, in Matthew 26:33, "Even if all fall away on account of you, I never will." And again, after Jesus tells Peter that he will deny Him three times, Peter says in Matthew 26:35 "Even if I have to die with you, I will never disown you." But in Luke 22: 54 – 62, when the going got tough, the rough and tough Peter got going! After the resurrection, it is finally the time when Jesus gets to speak to Peter for the first time, face to face, without any other distractions going on, in John 21:15-17. Now if it were me, I know I would have had something to say, at least an "I told you so!" I think many would at least have done that or even shamed Peter in front of the other disciples and told him what a disappointment he was. Some may have even brought Peter's commitment to the cause into question or simply just gave him the cold shoulder. But Jesus never even mentions Peter's brash, bold statement about not deserting Him. Jesus does not call on him to give an account of his actions nor ask him where he was when He needed him. Jesus did not parade Peter's failure in front of the other disciples, but rather Jesus covered Peter.

We see this same Peter who had the first-hand experience of having his sins covered by Jesus, tell us in 1 Peter 4:8, "Above all, love each other deeply, because love covers over a multitude of sins." Peter got it! He experienced a love that covers and does not expose, and he turns to us and tells us to do the same. The problem is that many of us don't feel vindicated by covering; we would rather pull back the covers and expose the whole thing. The sad fact is that I see Christians all the time being gleeful in the exposure of other Christians sin. We secretly rejoice when a successful preacher or pastor falls. We feel better about ourselves and our little sins when we see someone placed on a pedestal of perfection plummet to the ground.

God is very serious about us not uncovering people. In Genesis 9:20-27 we see just how serious He is when it comes to exposing people's nakedness and sin. Noah had three sons: Ham, Seth, and Japheth. The Bible tells us that Noah planted a vineyard and made wine from the grapes. After drinking too much wine, Noah became drunk, and in his drunkenness, lay naked within his tent. Ham went into the tent and found his father uncovered because of his drunken state. He didn't cover his father. Instead, he left him uncovered, and went outside and told his two brothers about his father's condition. Now Seth and Japheth put a piece of clothing over their shoulders, walked in backward and without looking on their father's nakedness pulled a covering over him. The two brothers that covered their father received a blessing from God, but the offspring of Ham was cursed. This story was not about someone lying naked in a tent, or a grumpy old man putting a curse on his son. This story shows us how serious God is about not exposing another's faults.

As a father of two daughters, I do not enjoy nor revel in the exposure of my daughters' sins. When one comes and tattletales about what the other has done, I do not respond in glee, nor do I rejoice in them being caught in the act. In fact, when that happens with my children inevitably, both end up in trouble, though usually the one that told the tale and exposed the other lands up in more trouble than the offender. Why? The reason is this type of action creates more damage than the action of the offending party. This action destroys a relationship at its very core and generates a domino effect of judgment. God is all about relationship, and as we have learned, love! And there is no judgment in love. When we expose others 'nakedness' we expose them to others judgment. We become a party to broken relationships and creating an environment of judgment.

When Adam and Eve sinned God covered them, and I believe He expects us to cover others nakedness as He covered Adam and Eve. God hates us uncovering the nakedness, the failure, the shortcomings of anyone else. In Ephesians 4:31 Paul tells us to, "Get rid of all bitterness, rage and anger, brawling and slander, along with every form of malice." When we expose others nakedness all the things that Paul tells us to get rid of spring up. Those that are exposed are subjected to feeling bitterness, rage, and anger. We create division between those for and against the one who was exposed that many times lead to disagreements, fights and even brawling. Slander of that person or persons become rife, and many times the story of that person's sin is spread by many maliciously with glee. We plant the seed when we decide to uncover and what will grow from that seed is usually very destructive.

So often I watch husbands and wives uncovering their spouse's nakedness to others within their prayer groups or among their Christian friends over a cup of coffee. It sounds spiritual to tell your friend about all the things that your spouse is doing wrong, but what you are doing is exposing them to the judgment of others. You are laying bare their nakedness and widening the cracks in your relationship. Go together and get some relationship counseling. Or if they won't go, let them know you will be going, but don't go exposing your spouse's weaknesses and faults with people that have no stake in whether your relationship succeeds or fails, or with people who only know your side of the story. They are already biased towards you and can never give you unbiased advice. Don't go and uncover your spouse's nakedness to your prayer partners. Yes, ask them to pray for you, they do not need to know all the details. Remember love covers! Don't uncover!

Continuing in Ephesians 4:32, Paul shows us the actions that are in stark contrast to everything he told us to get rid of in verse 31, "Be kind and compassionate to one another, forgiving each other, just as in Christ God forgave you." The Greek word used here for forgive is the word '*Charizomai' (khar-id'-zom-ahee)* which means to show favor to, to be gracious towards; it means to exercise grace, freely show favor and willingly bestow forgiveness. When we forgive somebody for what they have done to us, what we are releasing to them is the same grace that God so freely released to us in Jesus Christ!

As a child of God, I am a recipient of the fullness of God's grace, and this amazing grace continuously flows towards me every day of my life. The Word tells me in Lamentations 3:22 – 23, "Because of the Lord's great love we are not consumed, for His compassions never fail. They are new every morning; great is your faithfulness." God's grace, mercy, and faithfulness are brand new every day; they never run out.

However, according to the New Testament, there is only one thing that stops the flow of God's grace in ministering to every one of my needs, in covering every one of my offenses, in blessing me in every area of my life. There is only one thing that cuts off the flow of God's grace. And that is when I do not release grace to others. When I refuse to forgive others, it stops the flow of mercy and grace. As we have seen in this chapter, this choice lands me in a prison of my own making. If I hold on to the choice of not showing grace through forgiveness to others, I remain indebted to pay back my greater debt that I owe to God, which we all know is impossible to pay, so I remain imprisoned.

In Matthew 5:26, Jesus is clear about this, "I tell you the truth, you will not get out until you have paid the last penny." Now the good news is this, that immediately after I start to allow '*Chari-zomai*' to flow again, the moment I freely forgive, those prison doors swing wide open, not only for me but for the person from whom I have withheld free grace. When grace starts flowing again, it starts to flow into those seemingly impossible situations. I'm talking about situations that arguments, bribes, begging, pleading, counseling and all the preaching in the world could not change. The release of grace opens closed doors, doors that seemed shut forever. The release of grace restores relationships that seemed dead and buried with no possibility of resurrection. When we forgive, we are releasing to the one whom we forgive the grace of God that He has given to us in Jesus Christ. What a power we have.

We have learned that we have these amazing keys that many times we have not chosen to use because we choose not to forgive others. We put the keys of the kingdom deep inside our pockets and hide behind excuses. We tell God, "I can't use these keys because you don't understand what they did to me. You don't understand the kind of hurt they put me through. God, I choose to keep the keys in my pocket!" But God is asking us to unlock that door, to loose ourselves and them. He has given us this power, these keys of the kingdom. John 20:23 "If you forgive anyone his sins, they are forgiven; if you do not forgive them, they are not forgiven."

Let us turn the key of His grace, His forgiveness, and let them out of prison. The power of God's grace is the power to win the world and the power for reaping the harvest. The believer who proclaims, "I'm not going to hold someone's sin against them because God has given me the ministry of reconciliation" is powerful indeed! 2 Corinthians 5:18–19, "All this is from God, who reconciled us to Himself through Christ and gave us the ministry of reconciliation: that God was reconciling the world to himself in Christ, not counting men's sins against them. And He has committed to us the message of reconciliation." If God is not holding sin against them, then you do not have the right to hold it against them. And by us holding the right to hold it against them God has to confirm what we choose to do because He said, "What you bind on earth is bound in heaven." It is about time that we release them and let them go!

CHAPTER EIGHTEEN

❈

Healing the Wounded Heart

"The Spirit of the Lord God is upon me, because the Lord has anointed me to bring good news to the poor; he has sent me to bind up the brokenhearted, to proclaim liberty to the captives, and the opening of the prison to those who are bound;"
Isaiah 61:1 (ESV)

O ver the years I have changed my desktop computer. The computer would slow and become cumbersome, or just become outdated. I didn't go and buy a whole new computer; rather I would replace everything in the computer including the motherboard, CPU, graphics cards, etc. It was a brand-new computer except for two things. I left the case the same, and I bought one or two of my hard drives over with all the software I used on the previous computer. I did have some new hard drives, but there was important data I wanted to retain on the old drives.

For us as Christians, when we come to Christ, we are made new. The bible tells us in 2 Corinthians 5:17, "Therefore, if anyone is in Christ, he is a new creation; the old has gone, the new has come." The day I gave my life to Jesus was the day that I became new. He did not just upgrade me he made me brand new. He replaced the old with the new. My motherboard, CPU, and graphics card were all replaced. I am still in my body (computer case), but the rest is new. In Romans 6:6-7 Paul tells us, "For we know that our old self was crucified with Him so that the body of sin might be done away with, that we should no longer be slaves to sin – because anyone who has died has been freed from sin."

So, if our old man has been crucified and we are now new creations, why does there come up in our lives behavior that is not like Christ and does not display this new creation? Unfortunately, we tend to interpret through these behaviors that we still have a sinful nature in us that keeps us from walking in the fullness of our new man. We hear preachers telling us that we have two dogs fighting for supremacy within us, the old man and the new man, and the one you feed will win! But according to the two scriptures I quoted earlier, this is just not true! The old is gone, my old man has been crucified with Christ, and in the same way, our new man was raised with Him. "We were therefore buried with Him through baptism into death in order that, just as Christ was raised from the dead through the glory of the Father, we too may live a new life." Romans 6:4. The CPU and motherboard have been replaced.

Imagine trying to share that computer with two motherboards, the old one and a new one, and two CPU's each fighting for supremacy. Nothing would work; in fact, I am not sure whether that computer would even turn on. So once again why then do we still exhibit these behaviors that are not Christ-like if the old nature is gone? The answer to that question is on the hard drive. Paul puts it this way in Romans 12:2, "Do not conform any longer to the pattern of this world, but be transformed by the renewing of your mind. Then you will be able to test and approve what God's will is – His good, pleasing and perfect will." The way to spiritual transformation according to Romans 12:2 is by the renewing of the mind or the formatting of the hard drive. The problem that we all face is the unrenewed mind.

The reason I don't walk in the full expression of the indwelling person of the Lord Jesus Christ is that I have a mind that still has the patterns (programming) of this world embedded in it. It has been programmed with the traditions of men, cultural upbringing, ungodly thinking, worldly value systems, and bad habits created over years of repetitive behavior. It has retained memories from hurts and wounds from the past that still create problems even though I'm a new creation in Jesus Christ.

I am new, but I have an unrenewed mind. I have old programming. Now I don't suddenly get a brain transplant when I become a child of God. It would be nice if the Holy Spirit would just hit the button and type in c:\Format to remove all of our memories and ungodly programming. Then all He needs to do is download all of the revelation of truth from God's mega network computer onto our tiny little hard drives. We wouldn't be able to handle that; it would just be too much. Replacing that old software takes time, it's a progressive growth whereby the truth, Jesus said, sets you free.

The more you know of the truth of the word of God and the truth of your identity as sons and daughters of your Father the freer you become from all of the effects of who you are in Adam and the more you can express who you are in Christ. Paul uses these terms, in Ephesians 4:22-23, "You were taught, with regard to your former way of life, to put off your old self (the old programming, the old way of doing things, the old lifestyle, old habits), which is being corrupted by its deceitful desires; to be made new in the attitude of your minds; and put on the new self, created to be like God in true righteousness and holiness." My part then in this reprogramming process is with the help of the Holy Spirit recognizing what's part of the old, and then again with His help replacing it with what is new in who I am in Jesus Christ. So, the pivotal aspect of true change within a Christians life is not fighting with an old nature, an old motherboard or CPU but it is dealing with the old software and we do that by the renewing of the mind.

For most of us who know anything about the Bible or have been in church for any small amount of time know about a man named David. In fact, you don't need to be a Christian to know the story of David and Goliath. A tale told across the world. When it comes to this aspect of renewing the mind, David is a significant person in this regard. David is probably one of the godliest young men that lived in the Old Testament. You need to understand that so many of the Psalms that he wrote were from his early days as a young boy shepherd out keeping his father's flock. He was the youngest of the sons of Jesse.

You will remember when Samuel came to anoint a king from the house of Jesse he almost overlooked David because he was so impressed with the older brothers. However, in Samuel 16:7 God tells Samuel, "Do not consider his appearance or his height, for I have rejected him. The Lord does not look at the things man looks at. Man, looks at the outward appearance, but the Lord looks at the heart." After Samuel went through all of Jesse's sons, he asked in verse 11 "Are these all the sons you have?" Finally, David is brought before Jesse and is chosen to be the king. The Bible tells us that David was a man after God's own heart. But yet, David has one of the most heinous falls into sin in the scriptures.

As a King chosen by God, he commits adultery and then to make sure no one knows about it he has Bathsheba's husband killed, and finally he uses lying and deception to hide what he has done. We might ask ourselves, how can a man like David fall into such grievous sin? He was a man who knew the heart of God intimately, a man who wrote some of the deepest Psalms about spiritual reality. He knew the mind and the ways of God. We have probably asked this same question repeatedly as we see people we held in high esteem, men and women who to us were godly examples of what it was like to be a Christ follower, fall into sin.

We look at ourselves and find that even though we love Jesus and want to follow His example, we too fall into sin on a daily basis. What's going on here? We might ask as we read this chapter, "Hang on! If my old sinful nature is dead and I have a new nature why then do I, and people I have respected and even one of the most spiritual men in the Bible fall into sin? And many times, not inconsequential sin (in our perspective) but severe sin.

Psalm 51:6 David tells us. "Surely you desire truth in the inner parts; you teach me wisdom in the inmost place." In Psalm 26:2 David says this to God, "Test me, O Lord, and try me, examine my heart and my mind;" The Hebrew words for heart and mind are '*velibi*' and '*Chilyovtai*.' Their Literal translation is "test my heart and my kidneys." Though this may sound strange, David is not asking for a physical examination, but the Hebrew language used organs of the body to portray degrees of emotional involvement in our thought patterns. A good example of this would be the way we express ourselves to those we love. we don't say to our spouse, "I love you with all of my mind." Rather we say, "I love you with all of my heart!" because saying I love you with my mind does not have the same emotional impact on others as when we say," I love you with all of my heart." In reality, we do love those special people with our mind; our heart isn't involved, it's just a pump that pumps blood throughout our bodies. But we want to portray something deeper than mere mental activity. That is why all the Valentine cards are not decorated with brains but with heart symbols.

The Hebrews used the word kidneys to portray inner motives. Inner motives are the why behind my behaviors and actions that I am involved in every day of my life. In these two Psalms, we see David inviting God to test his inner motives. He prays for God to test and try him and that is what God did. He put David in a pressure situation that exposed the hidden things in his inner man.

The pressure that David faced was inactivity, idleness, something that as King he was not accustomed to being. For some of us, business keeps us from having some of those things exposed, but we don't want to acknowledge it. We have all heard of the saying, "Idle hands are the Devil's playground!" For others, the pressure can be tiredness, stress, loneliness, isolation or a myriad of other things. David should have gone to battle when the time came for the kings to go to war, in 2 Samuel 11:1 we read, "In the Spring, at the time when kings go off to war, David sent Joab out with the king's men and the whole Israelite army. They destroyed the Ammonites and besieged Rabbah. But David remained in Jerusalem." I love the last part of that verse, "But David *remained* in Jersusalem." What's happening here is that the author is pre-empting the story that is about to take place with David and Bathsheba. David stayed behind in Jerusalem when he should have been with his army fighting a battle. He had a lot of time to kill. It was in one of these idle moments while wandering around the roof of his palace that he looked over and saw Bathsheba, and most of us know the rest of the story, if not it's found in 2 Samuel 11 and 12.

The foundation I want to lay first is that God is a God of incredible love, and when sin in our lives is exposed, it is not to embarrass or harm us. This might sound like a contradiction to the previous chapter where I spoke about "love covers" but the exposing that God does has a different foundation and motive than the exposing that we do to one another. God's love is what drives Him, and He loves us too much to allow there to be hidden things from our past programmed into our mind that has not been renewed by the truth of His word. God knows that the hidden things of the heart are the things that will harm us and others more than anything else. These hidden things have destruction woven into their very fabric and will destroy relationships, people and us. God will expose these hidden motives so that we can walk in all the fullness of who He is. God is too gracious to let you get away with the hidden things in the inner man.

David told us this in Psalm 51:6, in essence, he says, "I had the wisdom in my head, but this wisdom had not changed me in my heart. I had the knowledge in my head, but that knowledge had not transformed my heart." "Surely you desire truth in the inner parts; you teach me wisdom in the inmost place." God is doing exactly that with us as His people, and it isn't threatening or scary as you might feel that it is. The only thing that could be very uncomfortable is if you don't allow him to do what he wants to do. Because God has you as a priority, he doesn't mind doing it publicly if you won't yield to the work of the spirit in your life in privacy.

If we remain in denial, refusing to allow the Spirit to change us for our benefit and others, then God who loves us too much to let us get away with something that will eventually destroy us or others will expose that destructive habit or behavior that is lying hidden in us! Unfortunately, we've had these horrible, devastating pictures of ministries crashing and burning and we ask the question, "What happened?" What occurred was that truth didn't prevail in the inward parts. The ministers got so busy in their work for God that they never allowed the Holy Spirit to change them in those hidden areas. They did not allow Him to heal their emotional wounds. They were living in denial, and even though these hidden motives would crop up every so often, their business for God covered over the cracks.

Christianity is an inward religion, but we get professional at doing things externally. We live on an external level; meanwhile, deep down inside us, there are wounds, hurts, rejection, fear, and anger. All these things are lurking in the bottom of our inner parts that we don't allow the Holy Spirit to invade and transform by His power. There has been a large credibility gap between our private life and our public life. The word integrity derived from the Latin word integer means a whole number. What integrity means is wholeness. There are many pastors, leaders, Christians that have not allowed God to heal those things that are creating this double living. Behind the scenes, we live one way but in front of people another. God wants to heal us so that we become people of integrity (wholeness) so that we are no different in front of people than we are when we are out of the sight of people.

Isaiah 61:1 - 2 says, "The Spirit of the Sovereign Lord is on me, because the Lord has anointed me to preach good news to the poor. He has sent me to bind up the brokenhearted, to proclaim freedom for the captives and release from darkness for the prisoners, to proclaim the year of the Lord's favor . . . " Isaiah is prophesying about Jesus. Hundreds of years later in Luke 4:18 – 19 Jesus reads this scripture about himself.

1. Though Isaiah and then Jesus was speaking about the Messiah and Himself respectively because we are Christians (little anointed ones) we carry the same anointing Jesus did.
2. There is a clear progression here about the way this anointing we carry accomplishes freedom.
3. It encourages and equips us to share the Good News of the Gospel to the poor of Spirit, i.e., those without Christ.
4. It gives us the ability to release healing to those who are suffering from past wounds.
5. It gives us the power to come against the enemy's power that holds so many people captive.
6. It sets us free to proclaim his favor over people.

I would like to focus on points 4 and 5 in the next section. Over the years in ministry, I have dealt with many who have been under the power of the enemy. I would come against that power in the name of Jesus and see people getting delivered from all sorts of things. It was awesome to see someone oppressed by fear, depression or a multitude of other ailments being set free from the hold of the enemy. However, many times after seeing them come to Christ, being set free from the captivity of the enemy, I saw many of them return to the pigsty, and I wondered why people couldn't stay free? I took them through deliverance; I saw deliverance take place, and then weeks—sometimes even days later they were back under the oppression of the enemy. The problem is that we have gotten points 4 and 5 out of order. We shared the good news of the Gospel and people's hearts were drawn to His goodness, and they were saved. However, instead of releasing healing towards those damaged emotions, and healing of memories and having the inner man transformed by the truth of revelation to heal all the past effects, we went straight for the fruit of those wounds and started dealing with them. We never applied the Holy Spirit's healing to the root of the diseased tree!

You first heal the broken hearts then you proclaim liberty to the captives. If you have a wounded heart, you will never walk in true freedom. In that specific area, you will always be vulnerable to the enemy because he knows the emotional buttons to press to get you to react. You will be living your life just like David, thinking you are doing great and then you will get into a pressure situation where the wound that you have gets activated. Maybe you get reminded of something that happened in your past, and suddenly there comes an unwanted emotion. Most times you won't know where that emotion came from that you are now suddenly feeling. The truth is that it was always there since the wound took place, but it hadn't been healed by the ministry of the anointing to heal the broken-hearted. God wants to take our hearts and make them whole. He wants to bring integrity to our hearts.

David's inner place was tested under pressure and in the story, he fell. The good news is however that God can still bring victory out of failure. He can still take what the enemy meant for harm and turn it into good.

Many years ago, at a youth camp that the church I pastored held, there was a young lady who had been brought up in a Christian home, but had got into all sort of alternative religions and cults due to a wound she had received when very young surrendered to Christ for the first time. In her mind, The Christian God had abandoned her. While visiting her friend when she was six years old, her two friend's brothers sexually molested her. The deep wound that she carried from this experience festered into hatred towards God for 'allowing' something like that to happen to her.

For years, she suffered from depression, suicidal thoughts, and bitterness. During an evening gathering at a youth camp, she came face to face with Jesus and gave her life over to him. Being an exuberant youth minister, right there and then we took this young lady through deliverance and for the first time in a long time she said she felt the cloud of depression lift. For about two weeks after, she was a different person, but the depression returned, and eventually she tried to take her own life. What happened? Unhealed wounds, undealt with forgiveness left the door open for the enemy to grab hold of her again. If we truly want to be free from these patterns of behavior we have to open up our heart to Him, we have to be willing to expose our heart to Him. We have to be willing to forgive those who've wronged us for Him to be able to heal the wounds. If we are not willing to forgive there is nothing He can do. He wants you to forgive from your heart, and there has got to be that willingness to say, "Lord I'm willing to forgive from my heart, but I need you to heal me so that I can forgive from my heart." These go hand in hand together.

Let us return to Matthew 18, and let me draw a picture as graphically as I can so that you can grab hold of the supernatural impact of what Jesus describes in the story at the end of Matthew 18. As we saw in an earlier chapter, the story that Jesus tells to illustrate forgiveness begins in verse 23.

Jesus tells the story of a king that needed to settle accounts with all his servants. One of his servants is brought before him that owes an enormous amount of money. The debt is equivalent to two lifetimes of a servant's entire earning power. It's an impossible debt to repay. Now, Jesus doesn't tell us how he got into this huge debt or what kind of debt it was, that's not the purpose of the story. What Jesus is illustrating to us is this, that when God forgave us all of our sins it was an impossible debt for us ever to repay. There was no way that we could ever have done enough by the works of the law or through obedience or good works that would ever have satisfied God for the amount of sin that we had. Jesus is showing us that God freely forgave us of our sin because Jesus paid the price. So, the master is now demanding repayment of this massive debt. He says to his servant, "Pay what you owe." And the man replies, "Be patient with me and I will pay you everything." Remember just like us the servant did not have the means to settle the debt no matter what he did, and the master knows this, so his master ordered him to be sold, his wife and his children and all that he had so that payment could be made. The man falls to his knees and begs, "Be patient and I will pay you everything." And all of a sudden, the master has a change of mind and says to the servant, "You're forgiven."

In this story above an incredible supernatural miracle just took place. For many of us we focus on the servant's unforgiveness which takes place later in the story, but let's pause here for a second and camp at this beautiful moment. Picture the scene with me, one second the king is saying, sell him, sell his wife, sell his children, sell all that he has, I want my money. I don't care about the emotional pain of being separated and sold into slavery; I don't care about the emotional pain of having his children sold into slavery. I don't care about all the hurt and the trauma that this will cause; I want my money! Sell him! Now, the king is legally in his rights to demand all that, remember this is a time of slavery, people were sold into slavery all the time to pay off debt, so the king is allowed to sell him to get his money. In his despair, the servant falls at the king's feet, and he doesn't even beg for mercy, he says, "Have patience with me" which was a ridiculous request. The servant and the king knew that time was not going to solve this issue. As I mentioned before the servant did not have the means to pay this debt and no amount of time nor patience was going to make any difference. We can conclude then that it wasn't the servant saying the right thing or having the right amount of contriteness or showing the king how sorry he was that twisted the kings arm to give the response that follows. In the next second the king is saying, "You are forgiven!" That is powerful, that is supernatural, that is not something that is a common occurrence.

What happened to that king that caused him to turn from being totally uncaring about a man's hurt and demanding total satisfaction of the debt in one breath to the next breath canceling the entire debt? There is a key word in verse 27, "The servant's master took pity on him, cancelled the debt and let him go." The word we are looking for is the word 'pity.' A much better translation of this is in the New King James version which uses the word, 'compassion.' In the Greek, '*Spludgitzomai*' (a horrible sounding word) is derived from the Greek word, '*Splunknoi*' (another horrible sounding word.) The word means lower intestines and translates 'bowels of mercy.' In Colossians 3:12, the same word is used when Paul tells us, "Therefore, as God's chosen people, holy and dearly loved, clothe yourselves with compassion, kindness, humility, gentleness and patience."

Let's revisit the image of the Hebrew and Greek language. Remember I said to you the Hebrews used organs of the body to portray depths of emotional feeling. Logically then the further you go down in the body the deeper the emotion you are portraying. One of the deepest Hebrew words is the word womb. For example, in Psalm 103:13 David says, "As a father has compassion on his children, so the Lord has compassion on those who fear him;" The Hebrew word used there for 'compassion' is a word meaning womb. "As a father wombs his children so the Lord wombs them who fear Him." It's used more frequently to refer to a mother, but he uses it about a father. He is not talking about the physical organ; what he's saying is, when a mother gives birth to a child from her womb there is an emotional attachment so profound and deep that David says that's how God feels about you. He has a such a depth of feeling about you, God feels deeply about you.

Now the deepest word in the Greek language is the word, bowels and it's translated consistently as the word compassion. It was the emotional reaction of Jesus to human suffering and human need. Many times in the Gospels we read, "Then Jesus was moved with compassion." God wants to heal our hearts. He wants to heal our 'Splunknoi.' He wants to heal the wounds that we have from our childhood no matter how superficial we might imagine they were at the time, if they were not dealt with then. (None of us really did deal with them then.) All of those wounds are recorded deep within our innermost being, and they formulate an emotional basis for some of the actions that we are involved in now. Have you ever wondered, "Why did I do that dumb thing? Why did I respond like that? Where did that come from?" It came out of your 'splunknoi.' Of course, I'm using it in the figurative sense as the

Bible uses it. It came out of the depths of our inner man where all the emotional wounds right from our mother's womb have been logged away, carefully kept and stored in our innermost being.

Here is the fundamental thing that I want you to hear. Compassion, that supernatural release of a God-like emotion is only possible to be released out of your innermost being when truth prevails in your inward parts. Otherwise, whatever is in your inward parts is going to come out in place of that.

I have seen this in my own life with my two daughters. Because of wounding that had taken place in me, many times when compassion should have been the natural response, anger or irritation would come out. I would see myself get angry or irritated when one of my girls would do something that I had told them not to do and then get hurt. Many times, I would lecture them while they were crying, pointing the finger of blame at them instead of sweeping them up into my arms and comforting them with compassion. As God has healed my inner parts, I've noticed that I do a lot more comforting than I do lecturing because compassion has replaced anger.

A young woman had relayed this story. Whenever she heard people quoting bible verses, it would drive her crazy. She would get very angry. In counseling the why behind this emotion came out. When she was a young girl, there had been a thunderstorm. In fear, she left her bed and ran to her mother for comfort. Her mom pushed her away and started quoting bible verses to her, instead of showing compassion, taking her in her arms and comforting her. When compassion should have been released an opposite emotion was created instead because many of us have religious reactions or non-emotional reactions inside of us.

The Holy Spirit wants to reveal the truth in those inward parts, in the inner man, in the broken heart, and heal the wounds in us so that compassion can come out of us in forgiveness towards those who wronged us. If opposite emotions flowing from our innermost being are the norm instead of the emotion of compassion, we will not be able to respond as that king and change our mind. There will always be the initial response when someone hurts you, but if you have been made whole in your inner parts, the next response will not be anger or bitterness but compassion. In John 7:38 Jesus said, "Whoever believes in me, as the scripture has said, streams of living water will flow from within him." The scripture continues to tell us that these streams referred to the Holy Spirit. This compassion that is released is not natural, it is supernatural, and can only be done by the Holy Spirit in us and then through us. When someone wrongs you, it is near impossible to try to release compassion in your strength. But with the Holy Spirit living in us, having brought healing in our '*Splunknoi,*' out of us will flow 'living water,' water that brings life to others. Few things bring life to others more than forgiveness resulting from compassion. Here is a powerful story that was related to me that illustrates this aspect of the need for healing in our innermost being.

A woman that had been in a traveling ministry for many years had been suffering from depression for at least two years. Her counselor asked what had happened two years ago to trigger this depression. She responded that two years earlier she had gone through a messy and painful divorce. The person relating the story told me that he had felt in his spirit that the divorce was not the issue. As they were sitting in the room across from one another, the counselor posed a question to this lady, "Tell me about your father?" The response he received was quite eye-opening. The lady shot out of the chair onto her feet and said through gritted teeth, "I hate my father, if I had a gun I'd kill him!" Talking about hitting the right spot, her '*Splunknoi*' was touched, and it responded in kind! "After the way he's treated my mother and my sister, I wish he were dead!"

So, the counselor started teaching this lady about forgiveness. I believe that the church has so many distorted ideas about forgiveness. We think if we go to God and say we forgive it takes care of it. We don't understand why we have continuing problems because we don't follow the word of God and do things like Jesus said to do them. We take shortcuts, and we wonder why we get shortcut results! After she went through the 'talk' of forgiveness, the counselor let her know that they were going to deal with inner healing. Together they asked the Holy Spirit to reveal the truth about her father. Remember it is the truth that sets you free. For us to be truly set free, we need to allow the truth to penetrate those inner parts.

The first memory that the Holy Spirit brought to her was when she was driving in the car with her father when they drove past a dumpster. A homeless man was digging through the dumpster looking for food and other essentials that he could use. As she and her daddy drove by the man pulled a broken guitar from the dumpster. Her father slammed on the breaks, got out of the car walked over to the man at the dumpster and started shouting at him, took the guitar from him and smashed it on the side of the dumpster and then returned to the car. She said to the counselor, "That's how cruel my father was; it had absolutely nothing to do with him!'

The counselor told her that now they were going to ask the Holy Spirit to reveal the truth in that situation because only truth will transform you. Truth in the inward parts will set you free from the wounds that have bound you and allow compassion to flow out of your innermost being. As they waited in silence, she suddenly saw Jesus walk into that scene, and Jesus walked up to her father and Jesus said these words to her daddy, "I understand your hurt, I understand why you are doing what you are doing." And suddenly the Holy Spirit unveiled her eyes to the truth of the situation. Now, this lady knew some facts about her father's up-bringing, but they were only facts in her mind. Now the Holy Spirit made them revelation in her heart because the Holy Spirit showed her the truth about her father's upbringing.

She knew these facts: he had been an abandoned child and spent many years living behind a restaurant under a piece of metal leaning against a wall with no heating during the winter. He would scrounge scraps of food from the restaurant dumpster. Those were the facts of her father's life, but suddenly the Holy Spirit showed those facts as revelation. She saw the hurts of her father through the eyes of Jesus, and suddenly there was a break in her innermost being. She started weeping. The counselor asked whether in her mind's eye she would like to go over to them. So, in her mind, she saw herself get out of the car and go over to her father, and say these words to her father, "Daddy, I forgive you, I love you, I never understood why you did what you did, but now I understand!" Amazing healing took place, and at the end of the session she said, "I can't wait to go and see my father and tell him I forgive him and tell him I love him!"

Here was a woman who at the beginning of the therapy session wanted to kill her father, and by the end wanted to forgive and love him. It sounds like something like what happened to the king in Matthew 18.

What is the supernatural thing that will release compassion in somebody who is full of hurt and full of wounds and can change them from anger and hurt and all the rest of it and transform them into being able to forgive in a moment like the king? The answer is this. When the king saw the servants hurt as greater than the debt that he owed him compassion flowed. Our problem is we focus in on our hurts, what they did to me, their meanness, their ruthlessness, their unkindness, their grievous words, and if you are focused in on what they did to you, all you will feel is the hurt and the pain of what they did. But because you are a child of God, and because you are a supernatural creation after the image of your father, guess what, you can see through the eyes of God, and you can see beyond your hurt and see the other persons hurt. God wants to come and reveal the truth about all those painful and hurtful memories that you have stored there that are provoking those damaged emotions. He wants you to know the truth about why you have emotional responses in situations that are so hurtful to others. He wants to heal you and set you free. He wants to reveal the truth in the inward, hidden parts.

Part Five:

The End of the Road –

A Place of Rest

CHAPTER NINETEEN

✳

Building Your Forgiveness Muscles

"Consistency builds your confidence, confidence spurs on courage, courage releases consistency, and consistency closes the circle of completeness." Orrin Rudolph

Weights and muscle building have never been my forte. Even when I was playing rugby back in South Africa, I never enjoyed the gym. I would much rather run ten miles than sit in a gym lifting weights. I still went to the gym because it was needed, but it never became an obsession. Because of this, I would find myself weight training for three or four months then stop for three or four then go at it again. The problem with this was that every time I stopped and then months later restart a few things would become evident.

In fact, the four most evident issues I faced were:

1. I found that I never started where I ended. In fact, most times, depending on the length of the break, I would have to start from scratch, as if I had never started at all.

   Every time we take a break from building our forgiveness muscles, every time we slip back into allowing small events in our lives to control our emotions and choices to forgive, we don't start where we left off. Most times we must start all over again from scratch.

2. My muscles would be stiff and sore just as if this were the first time I had ever weight trained.

   Your forgiveness muscles are just like real muscles, they need constant attention, or they will become harder to use. Situations that were no longer offensive to you will start affecting your emotions again.

3. The weight I was lifting when I stopped was never the weight I could lift when I started lifting weights the next time. I always had to start with a much lighter weight.

   As you exercise your forgiveness muscles, you will be able to handle larger events with confidence. But if you stop exercising forgiveness regarding the smaller things, those larger experiences will defeat you.

4. Every time I quit lifting weights, I waited a little longer before starting again because my motivation waned.

Each time you quit using your forgiveness muscles, the passion, the motivation to begin wanes again. Soon you will just give up and stop practicing, and then you will be back at square one.

I find that weight training is a great metaphor for many things in our lives, but I want to use it here specifically for forgiveness. I want to relate this ability to forgive like having a muscle of forgiveness.

Throughout this book, I have used all the question words to answer all your questions about forgiveness and unforgiveness. I used the what, the why, the who, the how, the when and even the where of forgiveness. I've talked about the *Talk* and the *Walk*, and finally I brought in some spiritual perspective. But one question word I have not yet covered is the aspect of which tools to use to help yourself to be more "Forgiveness Friendly." I imagine your questions are: which tools can I utilize to turn my forgiveness into something I do without even consciously thinking about it? Which techniques can I apply to allow forgiveness to become part of the way I walk, the way I talk and the way I interact with my fellow passengers on this human journey?

As a Christian, I have given you some spiritual insight into this in the "For Christian Eyes Only" portion of this book, so feel free even if you are not of the same faith or even if you have no faith to go back and read the previous four chapters. I believe Father God's wisdom works whether you believe in Him or not. However, in this chapter, I want to furnish some practical advice on how to build these forgiveness muscles in your life so that first, you become so strong that lifting someone in forgiveness is no longer a strain or a drain. Second, the act of forgiving becomes such an integral part of your existence and journey, that it no longer is something foreign or something you must force yourself to do.

Building the Forgiveness Muscles: Practical Advice

We know the golden rule, "Do unto others as you would have them do unto you." Imagine a world that lives this way. Imagine, as John Lennon sang, "All the people living in harmony." I believe that if people would live the golden rule, which is, (if I blew it) forgive me! And don't we all blow it sometimes? If I used one of the four weapons on someone, which we all have done to varying degrees, I would want the golden rule applied. I would want them to treat me with forgiveness. If that is true, and I believe with my whole heart that deep down all of us want to find forgiveness, we all want to be loved and forgiven; then I need to act first towards others and create an environment of forgiveness.

Awareness

Having flown all over the United States for the last eleven years, I've spent a large deal of my time on airplanes. I can't think of anything (travel related) more frustrating when you are sitting in economy, and the person in front of you decides to lie in your lap from the moment you take off to the moment you land. I'm a big guy, and when I'm sitting in economy, I'm already in want of more leg room. So, when someone decides to push their seat back as far as it can go, my leg room becomes even less. And I do not have the kindest of thoughts going through my head towards the person in front of me. Now, this is not a tirade against people who want to put their seats back on planes. The point I'm making is this: I know how I would like to be treated. "I don't want you in my lap; it makes me even more uncomfortable in an already uncomfortable situation. So, knowing this, unless I'm sitting in first class, I do not push my seat back on a plane for the benefit of those behind me. I've seen the seat phenomenon in planes start a domino effect. A person puts back their seat, so the person behind them is now uncomfortable, and now they put their seat back to get more room, etc. Isn't it like that in life? We get the seat dropped back on us at work, so we drop our seat back at home on our loved ones, who in turn drop their seat back on others because they are mad and hurt. Wouldn't it be great if somewhere along that domino chain, someone thought, "You know I don't like to get treated this way, so I'm going to keep my seat up for the person behind me, even though the seat was dropped on me." Suddenly the chain is broken, and a new chain begins.

You've heard the cliché, "It only takes one person to change the world." That might be true, but I'm not interested in changing the world, what I'm interested in is changing the environment that I work, live, love and journey in daily. I think sometimes we miss changing the place we are because we are so focused on changing the place we aren't. Change always starts where you are. If you can't change the place of influence that you are living in, forget trying to change the place of concern that is beyond your influence and ability.

Okay, please allow me to use just one bible verse outside of the "For Christian Eyes Only" section. I believe what Jesus says here, whether you believe he was God, or a good man or a fable is still full of logic and wisdom. So here goes, this is what He said in Luke 6:37 – 38, "Do not judge, and you will not be judged. Do not condemn, and you will not be condemned. Forgive, and you will be forgiven. Give, and it will be given to you. A good measure, pressed down, shaken together and running over, will be poured into your lap. For with the measure you use, it will be measured to you." Do you see the chain effect of His words? You do, they do, they do, you do! Push your seat back; they will push their seat back. Locked within those words of Jesus is the Golden rule. Don't wait for others to initiate; you give, you forgive, you pour, you do! What if everyone did it that way, would John Lennon's imagined world begin to exist? I know that is beyond our imagination, and as I said, let's focus on what we can change and not on what's beyond our sphere of influence.

Here is another cliché, "Become a thermostat, not a thermometer." Thermostats have the power to change the environment, whereas thermometers just read environments and give commentary on it. We don't need more thermometers. We already have CNN®, MSNBC® and FOX® to do all the negative commentary. Let's start applying that Golden Rule and watch our small sphere of influence change. And here is the amazing thing, as we start to change what we can our influence starts to grow! Who knows? Soon you just might be changing the world and who would have thought it started because you decided not to shift your seat back.

Time, Consistency, and Behavior

Building these forgiveness muscles, just like real muscles takes some time and consistency of action and behavior. One of the things I was told the very first time I ever went to the gym as a thirteen-year-old kid was that to build muscle, the muscle needs to be torn. The image of this was frightening to me. Why in the world would I need to tear muscle to build muscle? According to Sara Tomm, staff writer for livestrong.com, "Muscle building cannot occur without first tearing down muscle fibers, the main components of muscle tissue. Hypertrophy is the term used to describe an increase in muscle bulk which occurs when the body repairs torn muscle fibers." There is certainly more to it than just that, but that is what happens in a nutshell.

Since this chapter seems to be a chapter of clichés, here is another one: "No pain, no gain!" I think that's relevant for building muscle and therefore relevant in building forgiveness muscles as well. We have seen throughout this book that pain is part of the process. Pain enters in at the time of the wound and can linger until the wound heals. Pain also is part of the healing process. As you can imagine, to facilitate healing can be a painful experience as the bone is pulled apart to be realigned so that the broken extremity can be placed in a cast. Pain is also part of the development of your forgiveness muscles. If you want the ability to apply the Golden Rule, to walk a life of forgiveness, you must accept that pain will be involved. But here is the good news. At first, the pain is more intense and lasts longer, but as the muscles grow, there will be short stints of varying levels of pain and recovery time is a lot quicker.

I experienced this when I first started weight training. Even though on my first day in the gym, I was warned to take it easy, I acted like Superman. I did more reps and lifted heavier weights than what my trainer told me to. My youth-like exuberance and rugby playing teenage boy ego played a large part in this, and oh how I regretted it. The next few days I was in hell. I couldn't straighten my arms, my legs felt wobbly, and my chest felt like someone had punched me. This pain lasted three days, but eventually, it subsided. Besides the fact that I was supposed to do only one part of my body at a time, which I ignored and that I was supposed to start slowly, fortunately for me, my teenage body seemed to have super-fast regenerative power. If I did that now, I don't think I'd walk for a week! Once I decided to listen to my trainer and worked out according to the schedule designed for me, I still experienced tiredness, even lesser amounts of pain during training, but afterward, feelings of satisfaction from my weariness were more evident than any pain and stiffness. My body was adapting; it was growing stronger.

Every day you have a chance to practice forgiving. You can forgive the person who cut in front of you in the grocery line or the man who blew his horn and showed you the finger while you were driving to work. You can forgive the dog that chewed up your favorite Blu-Ray case or your daughter who gave you some attitude on the drive home from school. Our days are chocked full of weightlifting moments. Why? Because people surround us, and unless you are a hermit living in a cave in the Himalayas, then you are surrounded by people too. The beauty of being surrounded by fellow human beings is that they will give you ample moments and opportunities to practice those forgiveness muscles. One of the things I know for certain is this, hang around people long enough, and they will blow it. None of us are perfect and therefore are prone to say or do something, somewhere and with someone that will create an opportunity for an exercise in forgiveness. Our gym is life, and we don't need expensive equipment for this gym because it is filled to the brim with has the best exercise and weight equipment you can ask for: people, fellow human beings!"

It's the seemingly unimportant things we do every day that eventually leads us to success, but sometimes those trivial things can be the hardest and scariest things we do. In the movie, "What About Bob?" Dr. Leo Marvin, played by Richard Dreyfuss, wrote a book called *Baby Steps*. This book becomes the lifeline for Bob Wiley played by Bill Murray. Wiley is suffering from multiple phobias. At the beginning of the movie, Bob is trying to get out of his apartment to see Dr. Marvin. Of course, due to his phobias, this is no easy feat. After finally getting out of his front door, Bob finds himself in the corridor of his apartment complex. Bob Wiley is speaking. . . "baby step onto the elevator. . . baby step into the elevator. . . I'm *in* the elevator." [Elevator doors close] Bob Wiley: AHHHHHHHHHHHHH!

The consistency of doing the seemingly insignificant things that bring about success and victory in our lives is critical. Fear can hinder this and stop us from doing what we need to, but here is the problem, only by doing things with consistency can courage be released eventually. You see, consistency builds your confidence, confidence spurs on courage, courage releases consistency, and consistency closes the circle of completeness.

Look for those moments where you can apply the Golden Rule within your day consistently. Consistently releasing forgiveness will start to build your confidence even though it's hard and sometimes scary to do. The more confident you are, the more courage you gain, which leads right back into the confidence in continuing the consistency of forgiveness, which brings the whole circle to a close. The benefit of this is that a man or woman who walks in forgiveness of themselves and others are men and woman whose emotions and relationships are strong, stable and whole.

Just as I received an exercise plan when I decided to start working out, let me give you a six-step exercise plan that I would encourage that you place in your daily routine.

1. Stretch your way to learning to accept the truth about other's behaviors.
2. Ensure you practice your squats of personal responsibility for your choices.
3. Life is your personal trainer, search for the lessons and the gifts life teaches you in each experience.
4. Use the bicep curl of forgiving quickly.
5. Shoulder press your attitude of gratitude.

Step One: Stretch

Stretch your way to learning to accept the truth about other's behaviors: One of the ways to become more flexible and improve range of motion is through stretching. Some of the latest research points to the fact that stretching hinders injury to muscles. It gives people a wider range of motion in their joints and muscles. A wide range of motion can help us perform our daily activities, and improve balance and posture, which are important to prevent falls and other injuries as we age. In the same way, following a few helpful stretch routines daily will prepare you for those times you need all the flexibility and range of motion you can get.

Three Basic Stretch Routines

1. The ability to understand first before getting others to understand you.
2. The practice of expecting to be treated well but not being surprised when you are not.
3. The viewpoint of accepting that unfavorable and even hurtful things do happen and sometimes you can't avoid them.

The Ability to Understand First

The first stretch is the ability to understand first before getting others to understand you. We need to stretch our forgiveness muscles by practicing stretching our ability to ask questions. Seeking to understand why some people behave the way they do can help you respond to their behavior with a lot more grace and not allow yourself to be wounded so easily. These questions do not need to be directed at the person who is committing the behavior, sometimes that is impossible. Rather it is a skill that we can practice until it becomes second nature.

Remember most of our days are not taken up by the big, humongous, hurtful situations that can so devastate us for a lifetime. Thankfully, these are few and far between. Do they happen? Yes! But for most of us, they do not happen on an everyday basis. What we face daily, as I mentioned before, are the small annoyances, small hurts, and frustrations, sometimes by people we don't even know. So, when these happen, see them as your stretching time. The man in the car behind you honked the horn and gave you the finger because you didn't see him and crossed into his lane. Then you have a choice to put all your energy into your angry response and fume all the way home and think thoughts of what you could have done to make him pay. The other choice is to breathe and ask yourself a simple question, "What made that person react so over the top for such a small thing?" There are many answers to this question, and I'm not expecting you to be a mind reader, but what this exercise is accomplishing is placing you into a different frame of mind. You are changing your thought pattern from one of "I need that person to understand how hurt or upset I am!" to "I need to understand why someone would react that way." You are seeking to understand before trying to be understood. You are moving from victim to a survivor.

Sometimes when I have used this exercise, a situation will pop up in my mind where I acted in a very similar way to someone else. Once the action had taken place a mere twenty minutes before, I became the recipient of the very same behavior. When that happens, it opens the door for me to re-examine my behaviors and ask, "Why did I behave that way?" All of this moves you away from a primed emotional hotbed and gives you time to breathe and move on.

Reasonable Expectations

The second stretch is the practice of expecting to be treated well but not being surprised when you are not. I believe that every human has value and every human has the right to expect to be treated with dignity and respect. The bleak reality, however, is this: being treated with dignity and respect is not a given, and every one of us will have those expectations tested and sometimes smashed. When that happens, when we are not treated with dignity and respect we need to be already expecting the unexpected.

Hold others to your expectations to be treated well but don't be gullible in believing that everyone will do so, even when your expectations are clear.

You've heard the cliché, "Expect the best, but prepare for the worse," this is not pessimistic, but practical. For you to be flexible in all situations, you need to have prepared a contingency plan. There are very few things that are worse than when disaster strikes, and people have no emergency plan or escape plan. When that happens, people get hurt or even die. So, have a plan ready when people don't treat you well. Don't be surprised, work your plan. If I am in a situation where I am being disrespected or treated with disdain, or where people have said or done something to hurt me, that is not the time for me to start thinking on my feet. Decisions under duress are usually not good decisions. Behavior resulting from hurt or angry emotions will never lead you to favorable outcomes. Use the A.C.T. contingency plan.

A.C.T

Access the situation – Is this worth fighting over or is it better to walk away? You need to establish this line for yourself long before you get into situations.

Control yourself – No matter what others tell you, only you can control you. Have some strategies already worked out on how to do this. In fact, deep breathing, counting to ten and other such strategies are helpful.

Turn it around – Find something positive to say about the situation. "If that person hadn't blown his horn, I might not have seen him, and we could have been in an accident." This third part takes practice. It's easy always to see things in a negative light. Positivity takes practice.

Realistic Viewpoint

The third stretch is the viewpoint of accepting that unfavorable and even hurtful things do happen and sometimes you can't avoid them. Accept the truth that once a bad circumstance has taken place the entire ball of response (be it your fault or not) is now in your court and that circumstance is now waiting for that response. The decision you take on how to strike that ball will either turn you into a victim that will lose every time or a survivor that will always win in the end. The problem is that when these circumstances occur, we tend to become demanding. The little voice inside our head begins a monologue that sounds something like this. "This should never have happened to me! This was wrong, and I will not accept it!" The monologue can change slightly from situation to situation, but the basic premise remains the same. These events should not have occurred, and I will not accept them. So, what is wrong with that? It sounds reasonable. The problem here is that our monologue, though containing some truth has a dangerous lie embedded within it.

The truth is that we have a right to expect to be treated well; the lie that gets us into trouble is the all-encompassing statement that what just happened should not have happened. We use absolute terms, creating in our minds a belief that what we just experienced had no right to happen to us and therefore we can never find any peace within the experience. Before you get mad at me and think that I'm using the blame game here by telling you that what happened to you was your fault, let's take a step back and examine the premise. For this to work, you need to believe these next four statements.

1. Life has its own set of rules, and we as humans are not as in control of circumstances happening to us and around us as we might think.
2. Bad things can happen to us without us having caused them, instigated them or deserved for them to happen.
3. By us using absolute words and demanding that things should not have happened, does not change the fact that they did happen, and sets us up for major disappointment.
4. The faster we come to grips with what terrible thing happened to us and accept that it happened, the quicker we can find healing and release from the pain and anger that circumstances have caused in our lives.

The stretch is in the way you frame your monologue that takes place between your ears. When the finger is shown, and the horn has been blown, don't let the old script play out which would sound something like, "That shouldn't have happened, that person should not have treated me that way!" Which now leads you down the road of defensiveness, anger and even sometimes reprisal. A better monologue would sound like this, "That just happened and nothing I could have done or will do will change that fact!" Learning to accept and not avoid or demand that something should not have happened even when it's done and over with will help make you a much happier person when things take place that are beyond your control. It prepares your forgiveness muscles to be more flexible in whatever circumstance you face. It teaches you to roll with the punches.

Step Two: Squats

Ensure you practice your squats of personal responsibility for your choices. I dealt with choice in chapters four and five, so I will not say much about this in danger of repeating myself. One thing I will say, however, is some novice bodybuilders tend to train their upper body and neglect their legs. The reason they do this is that the upper body shows results a lot faster than the legs and training the upper body is a lot easier than the legs. This is a big mistake because the legs of a bodybuilder are as important if not more important than the upper body. Strong legs give you support and good balance as you are picking up heavier and heavier weights and help you exert more power in upper body exercises. Just like the legs of a bodybuilder, the strength of the legs of personal responsibility for your choices you make support you and keep you stable as you lift the weights of forgiveness.

The more you practice personal responsibility in all the choices you make and in the forgiveness situations you face the more power you can exert over your choices. The more you neglect training these legs of choice, the more you will feel out of control, lose your balance in times when you need it most, and you will feel you have no choice which will lead you into making the wrong choices. Re-read chapters four and five and remember, you do have a choice, and the more you exercise those legs, the more you will feel in control of your choices!

Step Three: Use Your Personal Trainer

Life is your personal trainer, search for the lessons and the gifts life teaches you in each experience. There have been coaches and trainers in my life that I have liked and others I've disliked. However, I have learned many lessons from both types. Sometimes the coaches who I disliked at the time made me stronger. I've changed my mind about them as I realized that what they put me through was not to harm me, they were pushing me for my benefit and growth. The tough training they put me through became a gift to me rather than a punishment or a curse.

Life can be a tough coach sometimes, and the people it throws at us can be a bitter pill to swallow. As we face some of these people and the situations we find ourselves in when dealing with them sometimes daily, we must start looking for the gems. In the valley of darkness across the valley floor are scattered gems of immense value. These can only be found in this valley and nowhere else, but to find them you must have walked in that valley and be consciously looking for them. If not, you will just see them as another hardship because they'll be cutting your bare feet.

Many years ago, I was fired from a position, and I felt slighted and betrayed, as well as furious at the ones that fired me. For a while I allowed bitterness and resentment to fester in my heart towards the people and the organization that treated me so badly. I felt that the firing was petty and unjust and that the real culprit was left unpunished. After my revelation about forgiveness and letting things go, these people and organization were some of the first that I talked and walked through forgiveness. Once forgiveness cleared my vision, I saw with more clarity the part I played in the whole situation. I saw areas in my life that were problematic and that if I did not work on them, I could quite easily be fired again and again from future opportunities of employment. This clarity of vision was a huge gift to me; it was a gem of great worth. It helped me from that moment on to grow and flourish in the very areas that were potential pitfalls in my career.

So many times, we are so wrapped up in our response or our anger due to what has happened that we don't see the lessons and gifts that these moments can provide. It is a learned skill to step back and ask, "What can I learn from what I've just experienced?" Archibald MacLeish an American poet and writer said, "There is only one thing more painful than learning from experience and that is not learning from experience." I agree. These moments that we face every day are small priceless gems and are so easily lost in the beach sands of self-pity and self-preservation. If we focus on our hurt feelings and allow bitterness to blossom, we will miss the life lessons and gifts these moments leave us.

Step Four: Bicep Curls

Use the bicep curl of forgiving quickly. During the early part of our marriage, my wife and I were not good at forgiving one another. When we had fights, which were often, especially in our first three years. We would not talk to one another for sometimes weeks. We would hold grudges, sulk and ignore one another. As we both grew in the revelation of forgiveness and we started practicing the principles in this book, the times between fight and reconciliation grew shorter and shorter. Until we've for the most part got it down to less than an hour, this did not just happen naturally, but with practice. Just like a bodybuilder does not get ripped biceps after one session on the dumbbells, so to our forgiveness muscles need regular workout sessions.

These daily experiences we find ourselves in are perfect opportunities to practice using our forgiveness muscles. Instead of mumbling for the next hour about someone who has offended you, learn to speak out forgiveness as quickly as possible even if these encounters are brief and over quickly. And while you may not be speaking to the person directly, the offense can still impact you negatively. So, when this happens, and you've followed the previous steps, then just under your breath talk the talk of forgiveness. "I forgive that person for (fill in the blank). And I release them and choose not to hold onto my anger or judgment towards them." This simple process might sound just like words, but there is power locked up in them. It channels your thoughts and feelings in the right direction and helps you focus on more important things in life than grumbling about someone you don't know, don't care about and probably will never see again in some cases.

As you practice this type of forgiveness, when the real hard ones come along, where you have more invested in the relationship that is now hurting you, you will find that all the small practice sessions will start to pay dividends. Your forgiveness muscles are trained and ready to lift the heavier weight. The problem is that if you allow insignificant events to keep you locked up in unforgiveness and bitterness, there is very little chance that you will deal with the larger more weightier issues correctly. And that will place you squarely all the way back into carrying all those packs on your back once again.

Step Five: Shoulder Press

Shoulder press your attitude of gratitude. We live in a society where the simple act of saying thank you is something that we seldom hear. A man I respect shared a story of how over the years he has had the privilege to take a few Heisman Trophy winners, a few top NFL and NBA players out to lunch. He noted however that not one of all these million-dollar athletes ever offered to pay for the lunch. Not one of them told him, "Thank you!" No, why should they? I mean it was the gentleman who took them out to lunch which really should have said thank you, right? Just for them to allow him to be in their presence and get to buy their lunch was thanks enough!

I hope you have picked up that I'm a little sarcastic. Entitlement and taking things for granted seems to be the norm in our Western society, not only amongst our superstars but even amongst our children and us. While teaching classes in a high school, I remember having to remind teenagers to say thank you for something I did to help them, or other teachers did for them. Sadly, I had to remind them more times than not. I believe learning gratefulness begins at home, and if parents are themselves not living an attitude of gratefulness so neither will their children.

So why is gratefulness the fifth step in our exercise plan? What does gratefulness have to do with being able to grow your forgiveness muscles? And what does gratefulness have to do with forgiveness at all? Have you ever heard the phrase, "They have broad shoulders"? Or "He has strong shoulders," used in the figurative? When you hear that, what does it mean to you? I believe for most of us it means, the person can carry more burdens than most, they can carry responsibility well, and most importantly, they are not offended as easily as others are. What helps you develop those three traits? What helps you develop your 'shoulders' to shoulder burdens with ease, carry responsibility without cracking and allowing offense to roll off your shoulders like water off a duck's back? Gratitude! Being grateful builds your ability to do all three of those things with ease, it allows us to handle heavier burdens, larger responsibilities and it helps shield you against taking offense and being easily hurt. Scientific research has proven six things that people who are grateful have over those who are not.

Six Important Characteristics of Gratitude

1. Gratitude helps you develop more friendships and stronger relationships with people. Saying thank-you or showing gratitude in other ways, moves the focus off you and your issues and starts imputing value on others. People enjoy being around those who are not self-centered and who show thankfulness.
2. Gratitude improves your physical health. Research has proven that people who are more grateful have lower blood pressure, improved immune function, and recover more quickly from illness. Gratitude also helps you sleep better at night which also improves health.
3. Gratitude makes you more patient with others. Research from Northeastern University showed that people who felt grateful for little, everyday things were more patient and made sensible decisions, compared with those who didn't feel grateful for the tiny things in life on a day to day basis.

4. Gratitude improves psychological health. Gratitude helps ease depression and reduces other toxic emotions such as envy, resentment, bitterness, frustration, and regret. Robert A Emmons, Ph.D. and Evan Thompson professor of Philosophy have both conducted multiple studies on the link between gratitude and well-being. This research has proven that gratitude effectively increases happiness and decreases depression. Research also proves because gratitude is a state of mind it leads to much more sustainable forms of happiness. A 2006 study published in the Behavior Research and Therapy found that Vietnam War Veterans with higher levels of gratitude experienced lower rates of Post-Traumatic Stress Disorder. According to this and other research, gratitude can help get people over trauma a lot quicker, and it makes people more resilient to trauma.

5. Gratitude enhances empathy and reduces aggression. Research participants who ranked higher on the scale of gratitude were far less likely to retaliate against others. They experienced more sensitivity and empathy towards other people and had a decreased desire to seek revenge.

6. Gratitude improves individual's self-esteem. Gratitude decreases social comparisons. Rather than being envious of other's accomplishments, grateful people are more likely to celebrate other's achievements and success.

So how do you build these shoulder muscles of gratitude? I believe gratitude is something that you can cultivate yourself. For the seeds of gratitude to find purchase in your heart's soil, you need to prepare your heart to receive these seeds. Long before machines could plow a field within minutes, most farmers needed to either do it by hand or by an animal. By hand, the implement used was a hoe. I have worked with a hoe from time to time, and I can tell you after a day's work in a field using a hoe to prepare the soil my shoulders hurt more than any form of gym exercise. Let me give you four exercises to build your shoulder muscles of gratitude.

Four Exercises to Build Gratitude

1. Recognize: On one of the many speaking trips I had to drive from my hometown to the airport in another city 40 miles away to catch a plane to Dallas Texas and eventually McAllen, Texas. As I exited my car at the airport, I suddenly realized that I left my wallet at home. At that stage, I had been traveling for eleven years, and in all that time I had never done this before. I had a plane leaving in an hour; my home was an hour away. Flustered and frustrated at myself I headed back home. After missing all my flights and having to reschedule them, I eventually arrived at my destination three hours late because of a stupid mistake I had made.

   I'm sure you have had similar experiences like this one where it seems everything goes wrong in your day, so why am I telling you this story? Because unlike some other days I've had where I have arrived at my destination angry, frustrated, and irritated this time I found that my heart was bursting with gratitude. Why? Because I chose to recognize the things that I could be grateful for during this experience instead of recognizing all the negative experiences. My wife who was seeing a patient but headed home and picked up my wallet. She met me at a gas station about 6 miles from home. My travel department who helped me to change flights (which could have cost me over $250 to change) helped me, and I paid nothing extra. I arrived safely in Dallas to catch my flight after a long drive. I received an E-mail during this whole event which let me know an amazing deal closed for me. And finally, I arrived safely at my destination.

I've learned to be grateful is not only reserved for good times but for the challenging times too. If we wait to be grateful only when things are going well, we will eventually stop being grateful at all. Practice the skill to look for things to be grateful for even when circumstances are tough, and you will discover it's a fantastic way to build your attitude of gratitude.

2. Write: Keep a journal of things for which you are thankful. Be specific. I know some people hate writing things down. But there is something special when you can see it in black and white. It builds those shoulders.

3. Share: Tell others about what you are thankful for. Don't wait until Thanksgiving to let others know. Tell your children, your significant other, your spouse, your friends. Tell them that you are thankful for them. Sharing your thankfulness is contagious and helps you focus on what is good in your life.

4. Surround: Surround yourself with other thankful people. There's nothing worse than having a bunch of complainers and whiners get together. Negativity is more contagious than the common cold. You have the choice who you hang out with. When you hang around people who express an attitude of thankfulness, you will catch the bug. When training I always found that having someone to train with motivated me more than when I trained alone.

The more grateful you are, the easier it will be to forgive others. Build those shoulder muscles of gratitude and watch as you will find dealing with daily offenses effectively will become second nature to you.

Work the five-step exercise routine and watch your forgiveness muscles grow. You will find that things that upset you and offended you before will have a negligible impact on you. And when you do get hurt and offended, you will be quick to deal with the offense and not let it fester and grow as it did before.

CHAPTER TWENTY

Let It Go!

"Grasping something with two hands shows purpose, commitment, and intent. Releasing your grip on something with both hands raised does the same!" Orrin Rudolph

I heard a story about how a certain African tribe caught their prey. The specific prey they were hunting were monkeys. The tribe would cut a small hole inside a coconut, just big enough for the monkeys to squeeze their hands through. Inside the coconut, they would place an orange or some other fresh juicy fruit. They would attach the coconut to a rope and then lie in wait. The monkeys would stick their hands through the hole of the coconut and grasp the fruit inside. Unfortunately for the primates, the hole was too small to withdraw the hand without releasing the fruit inside. The tribesman would sneak up behind the animal while it was distracted and club it over the head. All the monkey needed to do to escape was to release the fruit and pull its hand out of the hole and scamper up a tree. The problem is that it refused to let the fruit go!

I have taken you on a journey, a journey in which hopefully you have discovered more about yourself and why you sometimes behave the way you do. Why sometimes feelings and emotions that you never planned on have ruined relationships, friendships, and sometimes got you into trouble. I also believe that you have stared into the mirror and seen yourself. I am trusting that you made a decision while reading that your best option was to let go of your past, let go of the people that have used the weapons of offense against you, let go of your anger and bitterness and have chosen to grab hold of a future free from those toxic emotions. Like the monkey, if you choose not to let these things go even after reading this book, things can only and will get worse. Bitterness and unforgiveness do not go away with a wave of a wand. There has to be a "Talk and a Walk" to bring you to a place of freedom from the past. Grasping something with two hands shows purpose, commitment, and intent. Releasing your grip on something with both hands raised does the same!

This book has been about letting things go, but even though this chapter is titled "Let it go!" that is only the starting point. As you released your grip, hands raised, intentions clear not to grasp hold of that rope again, something else started to happen. You started to see a new rope, one that did not extend out behind you, but rather it extended in front of you and disappeared over the horizon. The problem with holding onto things of the past is that it divides your focus. No good runner would win a race if they kept looking over their shoulder at what lay behind them. If they did that, it could prove disastrous. They could run into something, they could trip and fall, or they could find themselves running off the track and going in the wrong direction.

My heart for this book and hence why I spent so much time dealing with it, was to get you committed to dealing with the things of the past, to get you free from all those heavy weighted packs that you have been carrying. But it would be remiss of me not to let you know that that is not the end of the journey. All great westerns and romantic movies usually end with the main character riding off into the sunset, or couple relishing their happily ever after moment. The end is when you know that the main characters are going to be okay. In fact, better than okay, they are going to thrive and be happy ever after. When you would walk out of movies like that, you felt your spirits lifted, and you are motivated and dare I say, happy at that moment of time. I've never enjoyed a movie that ends with a downer, an ending where everybody dies or lands in prison, and well that's that. I walk out of those movies unhappy, unfulfilled, and a little angry as to why I just spent my time and money to watch something that made me feel blah!

The purpose of this book was to get you to let go, but not just to let go. The problem with holding onto something with both hands is that both your hands are full and therefore you cannot effectively grab hold of anything else. You can try, but the problem is that your grip will not be that strong, as you can truly only hold onto one thing at a time. You see, if you were holding onto the past, you could never grab hold of the present and the future with much enthusiasm. Someone living in the past is never truly present, and if they are not present, then they can't see with any real clarity the path that lies before them. All they can see is the rope behind not the one in front. Letting go is more than just about dealing with your past, it's about again enjoying the now and restoring passion for the future!

As C.S. Lewis wrote, "Getting over a painful experience is much like crossing monkey bars. You have to let go at some point in order to move forward." Be it that you are an individual, or an organizational team, a church or a family who has been hurt individually, corporately or organizationally, the truth is that you cannot move into the next phase if you are still stuck in the last one. Letting go is also about grabbing on! You let go of the things that have been poisoning you, and you grab on to those things that are going to move you into a future of healing, fulfillment, and success.

My hope, my desire is that as you entered this last chapter, that your future has begun to take on a brighter perspective, that your present is no longer uncomfortable but rather full of new and beautiful experiences and that your past is finally fading away behind you. For all the Christians who have read this book, also remember that as you take your hands off your past, present and future, grab a hold to the Father's hands. And one thing I know about Him is that when it comes to you, He never lets go!

About the Author

Orrin Rudolph is a professional speaker, Marriage & Life coach, Pastor of Let Life Happen Church and host of the Vital Life Connection podcast. With his wife Sarah, and through their Vital Life organization they seek to restore vitality, freedom from pain and the enjoyment of successful victorious living to churches, companies, organizations and to everyone they meet! After moving from South Africa in 2002, Orrin, his wife and two daughters have settled in Longview, Texas.

Orrin travels throughout the U.S. and internationally speaking and training in companies, public workshops, and churches. Contact him at coach@orrinrudolph.com to bring him in to speak at your next event.

www.ingramcontent.com/pod-product-compliance
Lightning Source LLC
Chambersburg PA
CBHW060254100426
42742CB00011B/1743